Sponsorship:
How to get it and How to keep it
- an insider's perspective

Mike Turner

First published by Penguin Books Australia Ltd 2001 as "Critical funds: sponsorships in Australia and how to get Them.

ISBN 10: 1496016610
ISBN 13: 9781496016614

OBC Australia Pty. Ltd ©
PO Box 61,
Watsonia
Australia
3087

Cover design by Paul Turner, Pauly T. Design Studio

OBC Australia Pty. Ltd.

2014

Dedication

This work is dedicated to my late mother, Marie

Mum, your unconditional love, your guidance and self-sacrifice not only encouraged me to dream but inspired me to make those dreams a reality.

Acknowledgement

This book was written in collaboration with Di Websdale-Morrissey.

To say that Di's contribution to this work was invaluable does not do justice to the level of care, precision and consideration she gave to ensure this book was of the highest standard to present to the reading audience.

Di was instrumental in taking my clutter of words and ideas and helping me craft them into a logical and comprehensible document. She is an accomplished writer who was and is magnanimous in sharing her vast knowledge and experience with me and with those who seek her expert literary knowledge. It was a truly enlightening and humbling experience working under her expert tutelage.

Again, Di's contribution to this work cannot be understated: her wisdom and practical know-how were of immense benefit to me and has since held me in good stead for my academic writing. Her enthusiasm and professionalism shone through particularly in providing the topic material and structure for the chapter on the media.

Thanks Di, your friendship is and will always be a cherished possession.

Contents

Foreword

There is no doubt that the pursuit of sponsorship has become more complex in recent years, and that fundraising methods have had to become highly sophisticated. The publication of this excellent book is therefore both significant and timely. In *Sponsorship: how to get it, how to keep it – an insider's perspective*, Mike Turner strips away the mystique and unravels the complexities of sponsorship. In a domain where everyone is chasing the same dollar, he has delivered an easy-to-follow, step by-step guide to steer you through the perplexing terrain of sponsorship seeking.

Directed to all levels of fundraiser, from 'mum and dad' volunteers at the grassroots through to professionals, the importance of Mike's book cannot be overstated. From his experience both as a sponsorship manager for Carlton and United Breweries (one of Australia's foremost sponsoring companies), the Mayne Group and in his own consultancy, OBC Australia, he provides a wealth of facts, hints, tips and warnings. It is rare to see such information, from a real sponsorship 'insider', being made so accessible, and means that the existing public information on how to secure sponsorship funding has taken a quantum leap in direction and quality.

As President of the Collingwood Football Club, one of the oldest and most enduring sporting organisations in Australia, I know that sponsorship support is vital to the durability and stability not only of my club but of all sporting clubs, individual sportspeople, charitable and arts organisations. A strong sponsor base is central to the day-to-day survival of all such entities and a critical factor in their continued growth and success. The importance of Mike's inside information is that it furnishes a practical direction for your fundraising activities–a necessity in today's intensely competitive quest for sponsors.

Long before I accepted the presidency at Collingwood, I was closely connected with the club through my media duties and as a passionate supporter. As such, I was well aware of Mike's ongoing commitment to the sponsorship agreement between CUB and Collingwood. However, beyond the official contract there was always a great relationship between Mike and the people at the club. His door was open at all times to anyone seeking further assistance, advice or just a friendly chat.

I recall Mike phoning me after a junior football club (with which he had no personal contact) had approached him for CUB sponsorship. He wanted to help them, but couldn't offer assistance because of his company's strict policy of not sponsoring clubs with under-age players. So he had called to ask if I could offer another kind of help – to be the compere at a special event they were organising. I was happy to help and the night was a great success, with an impressive panel of top-flight sporting identities in attendance who had all been coaxed by Mike to give up their free time to help the kids. More money was raised in one night for the club than had previously been raised in the entire year.

This is just one example of Mike Turner's energetic and practical approach to fundraising. I heartily recommend that you keep a copy of this book handy and use it for reference as you compete for sponsorship funds. It may well provide you with the edge you need in your quest to secure the right mix of sponsors.

Eddie McGuire

Preface

Sponsorship. So many want it. So many need it. So few have any real notion of how to get it.

During the last decade, funding from traditional means has proved increasingly difficult to come by. More and more organisations – in sports, the arts and charities – now look to sponsorship as the only viable means of survival. Within the education system, corporate sponsorship is touted as the answer to funding shortfalls for schools and universities. The days when a fete, a sausage sizzle and a couple of chook raffles would cover annual expenses have faded into sepia images of people with rolled-up sleeves working together for a communal cause. Most of us now spend harder and longer hours in the workplace and no longer have the time or energy for such involvement. I also suspect that the proceeds from yesterday's fundraising pursuits would not meet today's escalating operational costs. We have become more sophisticated and have far greater expectations of our organisations than in the past. If a club's existence depends on its membership, and membership depends on image, image on success, success on being competitive and being competitive on available funds, then funds must be found.

'We'll get a sponsor!' comes the cry from many a cash-strapped committee. An easy solution or a pipedream? In the 1980s there was plenty of money, and those who approached the sponsorship table with a reasonable proposal usually went away satisfied. Sponsorship dollars became less easily available around the same time as many clubs and organisations realised that their traditional funding sources were no longer producing sufficient cash for their needs. This came about as sponsors refined their techniques for selecting sponsorship partners and took to evaluating proposals on the basis of changing corporate strategies and business requirements. After all, business is business, and the needs paramount in the sponsors' minds are their own. Consequently, the approach became more difficult – narrowed by the economic imperatives of the more frugal sponsor companies, clogged with people brandishing proposals, and littered with the corpses of badly made agreements from the days when money was plentiful. Dead ends and switchbacks appeared; other paths sprang up in an ad hoc way; red tape began to crisscross many of the paths; and soon the sponsorship goal lay at the centre of a maze that only the fully prepared and utterly tenacious could conquer. Today it is tougher still to strike a sponsorship deal. Sponsorship has evolved and the rationale and selection criteria for identifying suitable properties become more sophisticated. Companies demand value for money and will only attach their company logos or brand images to opportunities that can justify the spend.

As a sponsorship manager employed by large corporations and as an independent consultant, I have seen it all. Some came fully equipped and I sent them away smiling; others brought beautifully presented proposals with nothing of value to say and left empty-handed. There were the poorly prepared proposals with potential but nothing to support them; the supremely confident club representatives who thumped the table and demanded the world; the meek representatives who scuttled away at the first challenge. There were probably legions of people of whom I was not even aware, because they didn't make it past the outer reaches of the company. Few seemed to understand the system or how it operates, and without that understanding their chances of successfully connecting with it were significantly reduced. My response was to write this book–a guide book to take you, the outsider, in and help you to negotiate the Corridors of the labyrinth.

In this book I give insights into the company operations and policies that drive sponsorship decisions, explain the mindset of the individuals who control sponsorship, and teach you how to access the right person in the most effective way. I show you how to extract the best value from your organisation, prepare your proposal, make your pitch and secure and keep your sponsorship.

At the back of the book I have provided a number of examples of letters you may wish to emulate, a sample contract and a media release; a case study based on an interview with Mike Bowen, one of the most accomplished sponsorship seekers I have ever encountered. Every perspective adds another dimension so, in the interests of giving this subject more depth and breadth, I went to my current and former colleagues.

By interviewing other decision makers I hoped to bring a little extra wisdom to this book – wisdom from those currently on the front line. It is to be found in their own words in 'From the experts', at the end of appropriate chapters.

Each chapter finishes with a brief summary of the points it contains and one or two suggested research exercises. If you are really serious about making it through to the centre of the maze, I strongly urge you to linger over these.

This is not an academic text but a straightforward 'how to' book which seeks to convey vital information to anyone searching for sponsorship. I have developed it to appease the ghosts of thousands of hopeful sponsorship seekers who, over the years, beat a path to my door and were turned away. I have illustrated my points with examples from my own experience to demonstrate the differences between the successful approaches and those seemingly invincible proposals that were rejected.

The field of sponsorship is dynamic. It is characterised by volatility, changeability, fashion and caprice. Players come and go; trends come and go. But certain things are unchanging, certain approaches remain open, certain attitudes are rewarded. It is my intention that, with this book safely tucked under your arm and its contents understood, you will walk the corridors safely, advance to the centre of the sponsorship labyrinth and exit with the prize.

One

Sponsorship – a fact of life

Today is your day! Your mountain is waiting.
So . . . get on your way.'
DR SEUSS

For all those aspiring to access a share of the estimated 53.3 billion dollars (2013) that are invested in sponsorship properties by companies worldwide each year, knowledge is vital. According to the IEG (2013) report on global sponsorship spending, there was an increase of approx. 5 percent in each year from 2009 to 2012. The pot of gold isn't at the end of the rainbow – nothing can be so simple. It is carefully secreted at the centre of a maze to which only the fully prepared will gain entry, let alone find the centre and claim the prize. Logical and lateral thinking, insider knowledge, careful research and plain hard work are your tools – your map, compass and guide. But the prize is there and it's worth the effort.

During the last twenty five years or so, there has been an explosion of sponsorship activity throughout the world. It is everywhere; it can't be ignored or avoided and there are no signs that it is running out of steam, although it has become more focused, selective and sophisticated.

Having absorbed the names of sponsors – major and minor, consciously or unconsciously – we can rattle them off, along with the events, clubs, organisations or individuals their patronage supports:
- ❖ Budweiser Beer (2014 FIFA World Cup Brazil)
- ❖ Toyota (Australian Rules Football)
- ❖ Visa Card (last 10 Olympic Games – Calgary, Seoul, Albertville, Barcelona, Lillehammer, Atlanta, Nagano, Sydney, Salt Lake City and most recently Athens)
- ❖ Guinness (International Rugby)
- ❖ Victoria Bitter Beer (Australian Cricket Team)
- ❖ American Airlines (Annual A.A. Celebrity Ski Event for Cystic Fibrosis)
- ❖ Pepsi (Nascar, X Factor)

- ❖ FedEx, (philanthropic investments in: emergency and disaster relief, child pedestrian safety, and environmental sustainability)
- ❖ Louis Vuitton (LV Cup series to select the challenging team in the America's Cup yachting series)
- ❖ Barclays (English Premier League).

These marketing giants and a plethora of others, are among the huge assortment of well-known companies sponsoring sporting, arts or charity events throughout the world.

Most people could tell you that Coca-Cola has enjoyed a long affiliation with surfing and miscellaneous beach activities worldwide and that Red Bull maintains an active involvement in worldwide Formula 1 Grand Prix events. Some sponsorship activities are more subtle like the Ford Motor Company's initiative in Vietnam where it sponsors a Road Safety Education Month for schoolchildren; a TV game show during National Road Safety Month; and a "Road Safety News" program on the national Vietnamese TV channel. Heineken supports many sporting organisations and events internationally while Nike is synonymous with track and field meets across the globe – the list is endless and way too extensive to discuss here. But, you get the point!.

Through this constant exposure to event-linked advertising, which includes all event communications carrying sponsor identification and vice versa, we are conditioned to give credence to sponsors' messages and accept the correlation between their product and the event.

Sponsorship has become a valid marketing tool from the public's point of view. Some might say we have been programmed to judge any unsponsored event or activity as second-rate or of little significance.

I challenge you to visit any major sporting arena in any city or town and not find some evidence of sponsorship involvement. At the top end of the scale and to name a select few American examples:
- ❖ Staples Centre, (office-supply company), Los Angeles, paid $100 million over 20 years, home of NBA's Lakers, Basketball.
- ❖ Citi Field (Citigroup banking), New York, $400 million, 20 years, home of New York Mets, Baseball.
- ❖ Reliant Energy Stadium, Texas, $300 million, 32 years, home of NFL's Houston Texans, Football
- ❖ Philips Arena, Atlanta, $185 million, 20 years, home of Atlanta Hawks, Basketball

There are over 60 stadia of varying sizes and capacities throughout Australia and New Zealand that have assigned naming rights, for a fee, to sponsors. Docklands Stadium, a 45,000 seat arena, opened in Melbourne Australia in 2000. The first naming rights sponsor was the now defunct Colonial State Bank which paid $32.5 million for the rights up to 2010. During that year however, the bank acquired a new master having been taken over by the Commonwealth Bank. In 2002, the board then sold the naming rights for approx. $50 million to Telstra, and the name was immediately changed to the Telstra Dome. In 2009, Etihad Airway purchased the naming rights for an estimated $8 million a year on a five year contract. The arena name was then transferred to Etihad Stadium.

The above stadia and thousands of others worldwide all have in varying degrees, sponsorship signs on the perimeter fence, the parapets, the scoreboards and even on the hallowed turf itself. Down the scale somewhat are the hundreds of thousands of local sports grounds, arenas, theatres and art galleries that also provide sponsor recognition in many and varied ways.

For example, there is also an abundance of large and small horse racing tracks dotting the cities and country-sides of many nations. Outback racetracks in Queensland, Australia, (the kind of places where you would expect to encounter people who act and talk like Crocodile Dundee or the late Steve Irwin - the Crocodile Hunter), proudly display sponsor signage and logos – including images of brands, company names and motifs – on their finishing posts and at strategic points around their tracks.

On any weekend, junior sport players of all codes will run from well-signed dressing rooms in their logo dominated playing strips. Spend a night at the opera, watch a sporting event, attend a rock concert, visit an exhibition, involve yourself in a charity fundraiser – it's odds-on that you will see sponsors' logos screaming the corporate message from every imaginable vantage point, in programs and on merchandise – and, what's more, you will expect to see them. Such is my own acceptance of sponsorship that as I recently dusted off and watched a DVD of the 1970 Australian Rules Football Grand Final playoff, but something seemed amiss. It was the perimeter fence of the arena – not a sign in sight. The players' jumpers were pristine. Oddly, I found the sight dull (it troubled my sponsorship-manager soul).

Yet don't imagine that sponsor advertising is limited to the direct or overt. Browse through your daily newspaper. How many company signs or logos can you find that are not presented as actual advertisements? On one morning whilst reading the newspaper over a cup of coffee, I found that in the twenty photos in the sports pages there were thirty clearly visible and legible sponsors' logos and/or messages – they were in the background, on sports-wear worn by those photographed, on the equipment and even on drinks they were holding.

On three pages in the entertainment section, there were thirty live theatre advertisements which included eighteen prominently placed sponsor acknowledgements. Then there was the business section. There stood a captain of industry, pictured at a conference in front of a banner proclaiming the event sponsor. It's a powerful tool for all concerned, this sponsorship business, and worth the effort if you want sponsor support.

What can be sponsored?

The simple answer is - just about anything and everything, including you or the property for which you are seeking sponsorship!

We observe sponsorships hard at work in their various permutations everyday. Some are obvious and "in your face", while others work away diligently achieving the aims of the sponsors in a more understated manner. Below are listed just a sprinkling of what can be sponsored. It seems that all of the various avenues and means to sponsor are only limited by one's imagination.

Celebrities – Usain Bolt: (Puma - $8.6m p/a and $19m. p/a in total in sponsorships); David Beckham: (Adidas – reported at $160m over his lifetime, Armani, Samsung and Diet Coke); Brad Pitt: ($6.7m. Chanel No 5)

Music: Lady Gaga (Polaroid), Alicia Keys (Blackberry), Will.i.am (Intel), Justin Timberlake (Bud Light), Beyonce (Pepsi – reported at $50m), Taylor Swift (Diet Coke)

Cultural events – Montreaux Jazz Festival jointly sponsored by Manor Online Shopping, Heineken, Blu Win and UBS Finance; Hollywood Film festival sponsored by Starz Entertainment Group

Charities & Non profit organisations – Olympus Cameras sponsor of the 6th annual Fashion Acts charity auction that benefits people affected by HIV and AIDS

Government agencies – Lincolnshire Police, UK – sponsorship to businesses for crime reduction and crime prevention projects, community initiatives for children and youth, drug awareness and home security awareness

Universities – University of Manitoba, Canada (Pepsi), Ohio State University & University of Minnesota in the USA (Coca Cola)

Community – The Energex Company in Queensland, Australia actively seeks to sponsor community initiatives in the areas of safety, education, energy efficiency and the environment

Music Venues - Smirnoff Music Centre, Dallas, Texas; Carling Academy, Liverpool UK

Parades and festivals – Macy's annual Thanksgiving Parade in New York (first held on November 27, 1924), St. Patrick's Day Parade, Dublin, Ireland – Baileys, Toyota, Bank of Ireland

Individuals – Sarah Ferguson the former Duchess of York (Weight Watchers), Jerry Seinfeld (Acura)

Teams - Mongoose bicycles: official supplier to the Chinese National BMX Race Team until 2008

Sporting Events – Coors Brewery brand, Coors Light, was the official sponsor of the USA 2006 NFL Draft

Movies – James Bond (Die Another Day) - Samsonite luggage, Omega watches, Phillips heart rate monitor, Bollinger champagne, Heineken beer, Sony security systems, laptops, TV cameras and cell phones, and British Airways.

You – as long as your idea or property is attractive to your target sponsor, you have an opportunity to secure your funding if you follow the advice set out in this book.

A little history – sponsorship in 1492

Although the term 'sponsorship' as we understand it might have only been used in earnest for two or three decades, it is an arguable premise that sponsorship has been around for a very long time. In 1492 would Christopher Columbus have sailed the ocean blue without Queen Isabella's financial assistance? Being a resourceful fellow, Columbus realised that in order to discover the Americas and bring the bounty back to Spain, he would need considerable funding. As it was the queen who controlled the royal fortune, he applied to her for the funding to purchase suitable and sturdy ships plus the necessary provisions for the journey. There you have it – a fifteenth century sponsorship proposal. Columbus knew that Queen Isabella desired more colonies – and all the exotic spices, fruits, precious metals and more that went with them – for the Spanish Empire. He put forward his sponsorship request to Her Majesty, she carefully considered the proposal, then weighed the costs against the benefits, accepted the deal, and the rest (forgive me) is history.

Modern complications

Now, of course, things are considerably more complex.

Take, for example, the Olympic Games over the recent years, which have produced a flurry of competitive activity. There have been several media stories in which official Olympic sponsors complained bitterly about the ambush marketing techniques used by their competitors. Their rivals, wanting to connect themselves falsely to the Games, had pursued various means such as using well-known Olympic athletes to promote their products, or by playing Olympic themes behind their advertising blurbs. By these ruses, the rival companies were able to create, in the minds of their target audience, the perception that they were bona fide sponsors of the Games. And they accomplished all this without having to put up any sponsorship money to gain official Olympics-logo use rights.

By committing to the required fee to use Olympic Games imagery, legitimate sponsors should be able to safely assume they are purchasing exclusive rights for their product category. A high-profile worldwide event like the Olympics can bestow high-value media coverage on companies while increasing the positive image and prestige of their brands in the minds of consumers. However, dubious methods undermined the very large investments in the Olympics made by genuine sponsors.

Beats Electronics, manufacturers of the headphones, Beats by Dr. Dre, successfully gate crashed the London 2012 Olympics by sending directly to athletes special versions of the Beats range. The distinctive and colourful headphones were particularly noticeable at the swimming where athletes often listen to music to calm nerves before their events. They were also seen on many other athletes who were either wandering around the Olympic precinct or preparing for action at their own competition venues. Without paying a cent for recognition as an official Olympic sponsor, Beats drew millions of dollars in free exposure. All this was achieved at the expense of official sponsor Panasonic which was left flatfooted by the bold act.

After scoring his second goal, during the 2012 European Football Championship, Denmark's Nicklas Bendtner pulled up his shirt and dropped his shorts slightly to reveal a pair of green boxer shorts with the name of the betting firm Paddy Power printed on them. It was alleged that he was paid by Paddy Power do the stunt. Bendtner stated that he was unaware that he was in the wrong - he was just showing off his lucky briefs. After being banned for one competitive international and fined £80,000 by UEFA for lowering his shorts, Paddy Power agreed to pick up the tab and pay his fine. No wonder! It is estimated that the internationally televised stunt was worth approx. £10 million in 'exposure' to the betting giant.

Both of these examples open up an overload of legal, ethical and moral issues that only made the lawyers more wealthy and the sponsoring and sponsored organisations worse off for the experience. Such cases also result in sponsors becoming increasingly cautious and forcing them to prepare contracts that are increasingly specific.

For the honest sponsorship seeker this should present few problems, but as you approach the sponsorship maze it helps if you begin to understand the environment in which the maze lies. Knowledge is vital if you are going to be one of the lucky ones who win through.

The trouble is that today there are countless Christopher Columbuses out there – all with worthwhile and often exciting ideas – and the latter-day Queen Isabellas, the company sponsors, must make their choice from a vast array of enticing projects.

Competition for the sponsorship dollar is fierce, and only the strong succeed. Remember, however, that strength is not necessarily found in size. It can come with the right attitude and approach, strategic planning, timing, persistence and, above all, knowledge.

LESSONS TO TAKE FROM THIS CHAPTER

- ❖ Knowledge is vital.
- ❖ Sponsorship is a universally accepted marketing tool.
- ❖ Sponsorship is here to stay.

SUGGESTED RESEARCH EXERCISE

Rummage through a pile of newspapers that you have previously read.

Pick three, making sure that you have at least one broadsheet and one tabloid. Scan them cover to cover looking for sponsor acknowledgements, logos, banners, signs, and so on.

Note:

- ❖ How many did you find?
- ❖ In what section in which you find them? How were they are positioned?
- ❖ Do they appear in photos as apparently incidental background material or are prominently and overtly displayed?
- ❖ Do you remember noticing them the first time you read the paper?
- ❖ Does the number surprise you by being more or less than you expected?

FROM THE EXPERTS

- ❖ 'It is not how good your property is or how it performs, it is all about being aware of how to secure that elusive sponsorship.'

- ❖ 'Unfortunately, some people think that sponsorship is the exclusive domain of large big global brands. Not so! For many sponsors, little fish are sweet.'

CHAPTER THOUGHT

You may have noticed above that all of the stadiums and arenas mentioned above have corporate identities or brands in their names. There has been a steady and relatively seamless worldwide corporate takeover of stadia and arenas. It is extremely difficult to find major stadiums that have not accepted sponsorship funding in return for the naming rights. A review of stadium sponsors shows that the majority of sponsors are large corporations that are represented in the following industries: Airlines, Insurance, Beverages, Telecommunication, Motor vehicles, Energy and others

The rationale behind this form of sponsorship will be discussed in later chapters.

Earlier I stated that the simple answer to what could be sponsored was just about anything and everything. Although this is indeed true, the property being offered to sponsors must have some intrinsic value.

FURTHER READING

Lee, S. and Fielding, L. W., *The Commencement of Modern Sport Sponsorship in the 1850s – 1950s*, www.sportmarketingassociation.com/.../Session%206-%20Bush.doc

Coca Cola Sponsorships, (2012), http://www.coca-colacompany.com/stories/coca-cola-sponsorships

Mukherjee, D., (,(2009*Impact of Celebrity Endorsements on Brand Image*, https://usdr.us/usdrinc/downloads/Celebrity-Endorsements.pdf

2013 Sponsorship Outlook: Spending Increase Is Double-edged Sword, (January 2013), IEG Sponsorship Report, http://www.sponsorship.com/iegsr/2013/01/07/2013-Sponsorship-Outlook--Spending-Increase-Is-Dou.aspx

SPONSORSHIP FACT

Sponsorship funding is an investment in a business relationship that yields some form of commercial return to the sponsor.

SPONSORSHIP ROLE-CALL

Well, here they are! A random selection of household names, and a mere sprinkling of the thousands of companies and brands that sponsor an assortment of properties, events and activities on a global basis. How many of these brands do you see everyday? How many do you instantly recognise? Can you name any of the sponsorships with which they are affiliated? Do you use the products and services offered by these companies? How many can you name to which you are brand loyal? On reading each name, can you recall the company or brand logo and its associated slogan?

Kleenex, Jack Daniels, The Gap, McDonald's, Harley Davison, Shell, Mastercard, Smirnoff, Pizza Hut, Visa, Starbucks, Kia, Ralph Lauren, Burberry, 3M, Dell, Prada, Allianz, Amazon, Nintendo, Nokia, Caterpillar, Colgate, Audi, L'Oreal, Canon, HSBC, Amazon, Microsoft, Apple, Google, Coca-Cola, IBM, GE, Disney, BMW, Pepsi, Cisco, Honda, Johnnie Walker, Heineken, Pampers, eBay, BP, Danone, KFC, Anheuser- Busch, Nike, General Motors, Adidas, FedEx, Proctor and Gamble, Dr Pepper, American Express, American Airlines, General Mills, etc., etc.

Two

Understanding sponsorship

'Firmness of purpose is one of the most necessary sinews of character, and one of the best instruments of success. Without it Genius wastes its efforts in a maze of inconsistencies.'
PHILIP DORMER CHESTERFIELD

Let's begin our journey into the maze by defining the bilateral responsibilities of sponsorship. Unfortunately, I have encountered too many people who value sponsorship only as a means to a self-serving end. Their thinking, from the outset, is flawed. There collective credo is: 'I don't care where the support comes from – to get the funds I'll make all sorts of promises I know I can't honour . . . I don't care what the repercussions will be . . . I'll take any company's money to ensure my event is staged or my club is backed . . . I expect to profit personally from the arrangement and, most importantly, I'm not prepared to risk any of my own funds.'

If that is your approach to the matter of sponsorship, please close this book now – and thanks for the donation. As you journey through the maze, remember that sponsorship is a two-way street and must therefore provide a win–win outcome.

Be mindful, too, that sponsorship is a commitment by both organisations to deliver all the benefits and pledges agreed upon. Although most sponsorship agreements are legally binding contracts, sponsorships are essentially partnerships, built and maintained on mutual trust and understanding. If this concept is acceptable to you, you have successfully understood the nature of the route through the maze.

What sponsors expect from sponsorship

Today, companies are committed and expect you to be as well. They expect maximum return for their investment. If you are looking to secure a portion of the available sponsorship funds, start by acknowledging and respecting the reality that sponsorship is a serious and professional business.

There is at play a complex interaction of factors that makes a true evaluation of a sponsorship property (that is, any person, organisation, event or thing that can be sponsored) extremely difficult. However, companies have made it their business to streamline the process and in recent years have developed sophisticated evaluation procedures. Simply put, they can smell a rotten egg at a thousand paces.

In the survey of sponsorship managers that I undertook before writing this book, I asked, 'What are the most important reasons why you sponsor?' There were many responses to this question. The majority agreed that it enabled them to express their presence publicly in a market that in turn allowed them to sell more products and/or services. Several also cited the taxation breaks that a company can gain through investing in sponsorship arrangements.

Virtually all respondents said that they sponsored to extract some value for their companies. It doesn't matter what profile the property has or how attractive it appears to be, the sponsoring company must receive tangible benefits from the association and, importantly, benefits allied to their corporate strategies. Long gone are the 1980s, when most companies were in 'taste-test' mode. Then, the process was to select a small sample from a broad range of events from different categories such as theatrical productions, rock concerts, sporting events, individual sportspeople, celebrities and charity events.

Through a process of experimentation, sponsors established which relationships provided the greatest benefits for their companies, that is, the best return on investment and the best fit. In its simplest form, a short involvement in terms of time and money allowed sponsors to check out all of the available properties before zeroing in on a prospective long-term partner.

Things have certainly changed from that hit-and-miss style. Companies know that any property that can provide a large and loyal following offers an opportunity to target prospective customers and provides mass sampling and product sales potential.

Sponsorship is not a donation

The first step in your pursuit of sponsorship funding is to clearly understand the difference between what a sponsorship is and what constitutes a donation. Sponsorship dollars are investments made by an organisation to achieve corporate and/or marketing goals. These strategic investments are not limitless and come from the organisation's marketing budget. Donations on the other hand, may be essentially one off contributions of funds to worthwhile charitable causes. The donating organisation may contribute, because of their role in the society, where it makes good business sense to support community charitable projects.

Understanding why sponsors sponsor

Companies look to sponsorships to add value either in terms of building and maintaining customer relationships, instilling a sense of pride and passion in their employees and to provide tangible benefits for all stakeholders. The selection of a sponsorship therefore is not a frivolous act. It is in the main deliberate, planned and focussed. Most companies are extremely selective when associating their corporate or brand names with sponsorship properties. No serious and professional sponsorship managers will waste time, energy and their company's hard earned money on a non value adding property.

Experience tells them that the value in a sponsorship comes from its ability to allow the sponsor to build lasting business and customer relationships. A professional sponsorship manager will leverage the sponsorship in order to achieve the corporate goals set by funding the sponsorship.

In all sponsorship deals, the company bottom line is calling the shots: the deal must reflect positively in the sponsor's ledger. This being said, all sponsoring organisations support a particular property for a range of reasons.

To identify with a certain audience or lifestyle

Some companies seek to 'own' an event niche, such as motor sports, opera or swimming events and meets. In some instances, sponsors identify a niche market where there are relatively small groupings of consumers that are often neglected by traditional marketers. Even though these consumers do not form a mass market they can be attractive to certain sponsors. This may explain why French champagne producers (for example, Bollinger or Dom Perignon) sponsor elite events such as polo, or makers of rugged outdoor clothing (for example, R.M. Williams in Australia and Wrangler and Justin Boots in the USA) sponsor rodeo events.

They prefer to sponsor something that ties into their product so that their name and that field become synonymous in the public's mind. They aim to affiliate with top-level events within that category to win the hearts and minds of the niche audience and engage consumer loyalty. Going further, by close identification with an event champion they can foster a relationship with fans of that star.

If an event or property is a high-profile, well-respected one, that status is reflected onto the sponsor. In Australia, companies that committed to events such as the 2000 Olympics Games or the Melbourne 2006 Commonwealth Games were perceived to be benefiting the entire nation by raising Australian levels of sporting success in the international arena. These sponsors looked forward to increasing their current consumer base and possibly attracting and servicing new target markets by their patriotic gesture. Companies that committed sponsorship funding to the 2008 Beijing Olympics were not only looking to cement their status as international brands but also aiming to build marketing campaigns to secure a slice of the estimated 1.3 billion consumer market in China.

Some companies have been extremely clever in achieving their goal by implementing 'relationship marketing' programs involving sponsored partners. By building in a program where the supporter gains extra benefits when purchasing a sponsor's product or using a service, a dual loyalty situation is achieved: brand loyalty and loyalty to the supporter's club. Each purchase or transaction results in a benefit to the supporter, to the club and, of course, to the sponsor. The supporters understand that they are helping their clubs and themselves. Credit card organizations have produced dedicated cards with their property's logo attached. The incentive aspect, in turn, persuades members and supporters to acquire the cards and use them because the sponsored organisation receives a percentage of each transaction. It also fosters the image that the cardholder and the credit card company have a mutual interest and a common cause.

To increase awareness of the company and/or its brands

Companies use sponsorship for exposure. I have already discussed the proliferation of sponsor logos and signage. Companies will develop promotional campaigns aimed at strengthening their name and logo through an affiliation with an organisation. It may be that market research has identified a low customer base within a certain demographic which needs to be increased, or the need to launch a new image. Or it may be that the company wishes to remind the public that they are still out there and are still dynamic enough to be associated with a certain event. The combination of strategic on-site exposure and positive public relations results in a strengthened marketing mix, which can in turn be adjusted to maximise consumer awareness. And all this without a dollar spent on formal advertising!

To differentiate their product

Companies within the fast-moving consumer goods (FMCG) segment tend to use sponsorship as a means of differentiating their product. Within this classification are products that are consumed relatively soon after purchase, including food, beverages and the like. Most supermarket goods can be categorised as fast-moving consumer goods. In this highly competitive area, many goods are virtually identical at their core to those of other companies. It is up to image, packaging and advertising to set them apart. Sponsorship plays a major role in setting a product apart from its rivals and can become the real point of differentiation.

FMCG companies usually align themselves with whatever is currently popular with mass audiences and will look for a deal through which they can establish an exclusive selling arrangement. This is extremely important in a volatile marketplace. Often a shift of one percentage point in market share can have a dramatic effect on profits. If a company can sell products in the absence of competition, markets can be protected and share can grow.

Conversely, if a competitor gains an advantage through a sponsorship then sales and profit could diminish overnight. Such is the nature of FMCG marketing. For example, if your soft drink/food item/beer is the only one on offer at sporting events the profit-making benefits are obvious, as is the high level of exposure you will enjoy. Perhaps not so obvious are benefits such as the opportunity to mass-sample any new products planned for release. There is no situation so effective for this purpose as the combination of large crowds and exclusive sales. The information gained from the market research factor embedded in this arrangement is usually more valuable than the high cost of the sponsorship.

FMCG companies usually milk sponsorships for all they are worth, stamping their brands and trademarks all over the property to attract the audience aligned with it. Walk down any street and you'll see people proudly wearing company or event logos on their clothing. How often do you walk past someone who is wearing a branded T-shirt? Maybe you will see Lacoste, Nike, Stussy or a similar brand logo? In addition, key rings, caps, beer coolers – all sorts of premium items – are given away to the firm's target market to reinforce their sponsorship involvement.

At one time I attended a National Hot Rod Association (NHRA) drag-racing meet with one of my clients in Columbus, Ohio, USA. The magnitude and variety of merchandising items for sale that featured sponsor logos was astounding. It seemed that one fan in two purchased at least one T-shirt and wore it proudly as they cheered their heroes roaring down the track. When you consider that each event on the NHRA calendar hosts over one hundred thousand spectators, sales are not inconsiderable. Add to the T-shirts, posters, die-cast models, caps and other items and the total equals millions of sponsor logos in the hands of fanatical drag-racing supporters. It doesn't end there. The NHR A has approx. 80,000 members and attendances at all meetings scheduled in the USA in a given year total an average of 2.2 million fans. You can see why sponsors queue up to support this sport.

Understand that there are different philosophies

Whether you are looking for a sponsor for a charitable institution, an arts body or a sporting organisation, understand that some segments will be more amenable to your approach than others because of the potential the relationship would offer to create greater sales opportunities. The signing of an event or sports sponsorship is usually accompanied by as much fanfare as the parties can squeeze out of the occasion. Depending on the size of the deal and the parties concerned, there may be widely circulated press releases attracting the full media spotlight. The sponsoring company receives as much positive attention from the media as the sponsored body – a highly desirable outcome for most companies, because increased public awareness means increased sales.

The event organisers will want to signal to the public that a well-respected company or brand name considers their club or charity not simply viable, but a winner worth backing. With a major sponsor on board, other sponsors will follow. These new sponsors use the logic that if a company the size and reach of "X" has faith in you, then you are worth supporting.

Where agreements to sponsor charitable and arts organizations are made, there is usually little of this 'blanket' publicity. To attach the sort of hype and hoopla associated with commercial ventures to philanthropic deeds could be considered crass and might well frustrate the outcomes sought from the agreement in the first place. The objectives in such a situation are more general and less immediate. The sponsorship should signal to the world that this company is a 'good corporate citizen', one that is willing to put something back into the community that has provided its profits. It also sends a subtle message to employees, customers and shareholders that this company is worthy of their efforts and respect. The approval of these stakeholders enhances the company's corporate image.

Relative bargaining positions

'Sponsorship' conjures up the notion of civilised and considered negotiations where all parties have a set role: the potential sponsor holds all the cards and those who would be sponsored show due deference and agree to whatever is offered. This thinking can put you on the back foot and make you reluctant to approach a would-be sponsor. Keep in mind that sponsors are under pressure too. They must keep their product's profile up and establish, then retain, marketplace prominence. All of this can work to your advantage.

At Australian based Carlton and United Breweries (CUB) (renamed The Fosters Brewing Group and now owned by Miller SAB) where I worked, the pressure was full-on most of the time but became almost overwhelming during periods of intense competitive attack from rival companies such as Tooth, XXXX, Swan and Tooheys.

During the Australian 'beer wars' of the mid-1980s, XXXX beer from the northern state of Queensland took the fight right up to its southern Victorian State -based competitor, supporting its advertising and pricing strategies with a major thrust at securing some of the plum sponsorships in the state of Victoria. The Queensland 'interloper' even dared to sponsor CUB's jewel in the crown: AFL football. They achieved this by acquiring a deal to sponsor goal umpires and the goalposts. Brand logos on the umpire's coats and on the posts presented XXXX with invaluable television coverage and priceless exposure to potential consumers.

This, of course, raised the ante for sponsorship properties; Tooheys were prepared to disburse more than the sum CUB had appraised the events to be worth. Many events sold CUB products exclusively anyway and the rationale had been: Why pay when the company has a monopoly already?

Among these properties were high-profile events and organizations that were not considered, during the preceding period of relative calm, to be of strategic significance. When the 'war' began, they were therefore unsponsored and open to the advances of the northern raider. The reality of stiff competition often forces the most rigid of company policies to change. A swift and decisive policy shift by CUB would deny Tooheys a foothold in the state. When such a foothold would deliver sampling and sales opportunities, reaction was immediate. The result for CUB was a hastily developed policy of offering to bring all the strategic 'loose' sponsorships under CUB patronage to cut Tooheys' opportunities.

Again, sponsored organisations were the beneficiaries, as both brewers raced to tie up as many as possible, outbidding each other for the privilege. This was not an isolated case, and is a scenario played out somewhere in the world by rivals using sponsorship as a lever to gain market share. This quite normal business practice is driven by market imperatives, and while it sounds like a reaction born of panic and executed in haste, the companies simply acted as their relative positions and goals required.

Hills and valleys

This is a timely point at which to introduce what I have termed the 'hills and valleys' model of sponsorship (see Figures 1 and 2). I explain it this way. Imagine yourself on a hilltop, holding the high ground while your target organisation is in a valley. Whoever occupies the higher position can reasonably dictate the terms.

Before the 'beer wars', CUB was firmly established on the prime hilltop. Below, in the 'valley', were all those organisations and events that approached the peak, cap in hand, to ask for sponsorship. The war reversed these positions. Former supplicants now held the peak as two powerful rivals fought for their favours in the valley below. Messengers would appear at the door from time to time with promises from one brewer or the other – promises of money and offers to give them the world for their allegiance.

Where sponsors find themselves under some form of commercial threat, they will often seek out properties that could provide them with a competitive edge in their markets. Here your negotiating power is strong, as several firms may vie to sponsor you. You will find that in these situations there will be little resistance to your asking fee or to your conditions of sponsorship.

When approaching a company for sponsorship while you occupy the hilltop, your negotiating muscle is strong and generally your target will agree to your offer without too much resistance. Conversely, when your target has little or no competition, or has the major share of the market segment, you are standing in the valley, craning to glimpse the heights. Your target may be quite happy to sponsor your organisation for reasons other than competition or market strategy, but there is no real sense of urgency as the target has little to fear from its rivals.

Figure 2.1: Hills and valleys model where you hold the dominant position.

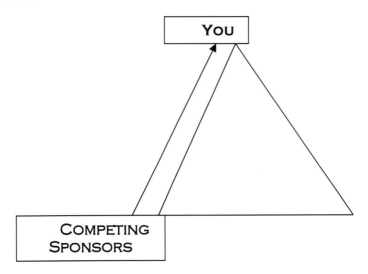

You have to work hard in the valley. You must spend time and effort presenting, selling and negotiating your case. The 'hills and valleys' principle teaches the need to be ever-alert to the market, scanning for those companies in highly competitive situations or faced with a new entrant into their market. Understanding and analysing these situations may direct you towards a potential new sponsor with open arms and a deep purse.

The sponsor holds the high ground. You have to utilise all of your skills and knowledge to approach and interest this sponsor. Here you are one among many and must work hard to ensure that your pitch has every opportunity of gaining your target's interest and attention.

Figure 2.2: Hills and valleys model where the sponsor is in the dominant position.

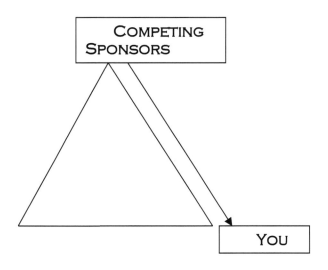

What are the most important reasons you sponsor?

- ❖ 'to gain marketplace credibility among customers'
- ❖ 'to provide exposure across all demographic areas for our brands'
- ❖ 'to create a strategic advantage over competitors'
- ❖ 'to prove to the world at large that we care for the environment'
- ❖ 'to ensure the long-term viability of my company and its brands'

LESSONS TO TAKE FROM THIS CHAPTER

- ❖ Companies use sponsorships to achieve a competitive edge.
- ❖ You must have something to offer that has obvious benefit for your target sponsor.
- ❖ Appreciate the 'hills and valleys' concept
- ❖ Always consider your relative position before going to the bargaining table.

SUGGESTED RESEARCH EXERCISE

List the companies you plan to target and ask of each:
1. What are the current pressures on them?
2. Are they operating from a valley or a hilltop? What factors prove this?

FURTHER READING

Below is an extensive list of articles that discuss Understanding Sponsorship for both the corporate perspective and the Sponsorship seeker point of view. They are well worth reading:

Copeland, R., Frisby, W., & McCarville, R. (1996). Understanding the Sport Sponsorship Process From a Corporate Perspective. *Journal of Sport Management, 10*(1).

Meenaghan, T. (2001). Understanding sponsorship effects. *Psychology & Marketing, 18*(2), 95-122.

Cornwell, T. B., Roy, D. P., & Roy, D. P. (2001). Exploring managers' perceptions of the impact of sponsorship on brand equity. *Journal of Advertising, 30*(2), 41-51.

Hickman, T. M., Lawrence, K. E., & Ward, J. C. (2005). A social identities perspective on the effects of corporate sport sponsorship on employees. *Sport Marketing Quarterly, 14*(3), 148-157.

Fahy, J., Farrelly, F., & Quester, P. (2004). Competitive advantage through sponsorship: A conceptual model and research propositions. *European Journal of Marketing, 38*(8), 1013-1030.

Cornwall, T. B. (2008). State of art and science in sponsorship-linked marketing. *Journal of Advertising, 37*(3), 41-55.

Collett, P., & Fenton, W. (2011). *The Sponsorship Handbook: Essential Tools, Tips and Techniques for Sponsors and Sponsorship Seekers.* John Wiley & Sons.

Brennan, L., Binney, W., & Brady, E. (2012). The raising of corporate sponsorship: A behavioral study. *Journal of Nonprofit & Public Sector Marketing, 24*(3), 222-237.

SPONSORSHIP FACT

Coca-Cola is "the longest continuous sponsorship partner of the Olympic Games. The company began its involvement in the Amsterdam games of 1928 and has extended its Olympic sponsorship to 2020. A total partnership of almost 100 years.

Three

The first steps

'In the morning be first up, and in the evening last to go to bed, for they that sleep catch no fish.'
ENGLISH PROVERB

Today's sponsors have become savvy and adept at choosing the most suitable partners that not only have the right 'fit' for the company's corporate vision but that can also enhance its image among consumers. Their selection process is sophisticated and finely tuned. They also offer different levels of support and will choose to offer their money to some, yet close the door on others. Sponsors know what they are looking for and chose one property over another for all sorts of reasons. You should recognise these facts and not waste your valuable time going up blind alleys. But before you consider the practices of potential sponsors, you must rigorously examine your own.

Before seeking a sponsor

Know your own organisation

Our maze is not for the faint-hearted, nor is it for the ill-prepared. 'Ill-prepared' is quite different from 'not prepared' and can in many ways be more dangerous. If you have developed poor practices over time, they will be the model you will naturally follow and change will be harder to effect. A thorough and candid assessment of your situation will expose any poorly thought-out plans, preparations, or techniques that may be holding your organization back from reaching its full potential.

Question all facets of your sponsorship strategy. Start at the basics. These are often so entrenched that it does not occur to anyone to examine or question them:
- ❖ What is your organisation's ethos?
- ❖ Do you have a 'mission statement'? (This is a statement of

purpose distinguishing you from similar organisations.) Is it clear in its descriptions of your priorities and, most importantly, your values.

- ❖ How is your organisation run, organised and administered?
- ❖ Are there policy guidelines relating to general conduct and administration, and to sponsors and sponsorship?
- ❖ Do you have a system in place for acquiring sponsorship, or do you have an unspoken policy of waiting for sponsors to approach you?
- ❖ Perhaps most importantly, is your operation run along professional lines or does it simply chug along under the steam of a few faithful volunteers?
- ❖ Worse still, is it a runaway train headed for derailment?

Have a sponsorship policy

Always keep in mind that getting the sponsorship 'fit' right is a bilateral affair. When you are looking at the maze as an outsider you may feel that a dollar is a dollar after all, and any dollar is a good dollar, but if you and your target sponsor have opposing philosophies or have different goals in mind, then neither of you will benefit from an alliance. If the issue is forced, the relationship will suffer as the different standpoints rub against each other, causing uncomfortable friction all round. If half your committee resigns or your members walk out in protest at your choice of sponsor, your celebration at gaining that sponsor will be an empty affair at best.

Here is a case in point. Several years ago, I was chasing properties in an effort to lock a competitor out of the picture. In my enthusiasm I offered a sponsorship deal to a netball association. I received a polite 'Thanks but no thanks': the netballers didn't want my company's financial support.

Identifying potential targets

Take a minute to list all the products either used by your organisation or sold at your events. Rank your list from the highest sale or usage to the lowest (see Figure 3). In this way you can identify target companies who would respond to your use of product sales as a lever during negotiations.

How to draw up an initial target sponsor list

Once you have a complete picture of your organisation and the benefits you have to offer (we will do this exercise in depth in Chapter Five), you will be in a position to target sponsors. The companies you approach will usually need valid commercial reasons for supporting you. Your task is to distinguish those companies most likely to find those reasons – companies that can identify with you.

Several years ago, the Australian company, National Foods, through its brand Pura Light Start milk, sponsored Australian Olympic swimming champion, Kieren Perkins who won gold in the 1500m freestyle at the 1996 Atlanta Olympics. Why?

Let's look at the strategy behind this sponsorship. Kieren Perkins is, (and was at the time the advert ran), a likeable clean-cut young man who was also an enduring and successful athlete. Pura Light Start milk is a low-fat product aimed at consumers with healthy lifestyles. I am sure the target consumers identified with Kieren as a healthy and fit Aussie. They also believed that Pura Light Start was a product suitable for their consumption, being low in fat without compromising on taste. The fit between sponsor and property appeared to be perfect. Added to the equation was a very clever television advertisement featuring old family footage of Kieren as a small child drinking his milk, and the result was a union that paid dividends for both parties.

You must also think in this way. Look for products and services that can benefit from an association with you so that you will both gain from the alliance. Be consistent in your quest and ensure that this is one of the main criteria by which you will not only seek out but also attract sponsors. The matching process can reveal a list of potential sponsors that you may never have considered had you not completed the exercise. Are there potential sponsors for your organisation from within the small list provided below?

- ❖ manufacturing companies:
    - o food and beverages, textiles, apparel, wood/paper products, publishing, printing, chemicals, rubber, petroleum, building products, medical supplies, motor vehicles, furniture, electronics
- ❖ construction industry
- ❖ wholesale and retail
- ❖ hotels and restaurants
- ❖ transport, storage and communications
- ❖ financial institutions
- ❖ real estate firms
- ❖ entertainment, motion pictures, amusements and recreation services
- ❖ agriculture, forestry and fishing

❖ mining

The answer to the above question is almost certainly a resounding 'yes'. After simply glancing at the list you should be able to think of potential sponsors from within many categories.

Lessons to take from this chapter

❖ Acknowledge that your event or property will match the strategies of some target sponsors but not others. Understand why.
❖ Sponsors can be found anywhere, from the largest corporations to one-man-band companies to philanthropic individuals.
❖ Determine your organisation's sponsorship policy and its 'no-go zone'.
❖ Consider the suppliers of products you already either use or sell.
❖ Always consider the question, How can sponsoring our organization help this company's bottom line?

SUGGESTED RESEARCH EXERCISE

To put together a rudimentary sponsorship policy:

❖ Draw up a 'yes' and 'no' category list based on these questions:
   o What are the values of your organisation?
   o What image are you attempting to project? Which product categories best fit your values and image?
   o Which areas of business or companies will you never be involved with?
   o Which product or service categories will your members feel comfortable about being associated with, and which will they not?

❖ Ask other members of your organisation to complete the same exercise and then compare the lists.
   o Where are the similarities?
   o Are there glaring differences?
   o Ask the others to clarify points of difference and their rationale for selection.
   o Throw them a hypothetical: If one of their 'no' companies offered a great deal of money to your organisation, would their answer still be 'no'?
   o Work through any problems until you have a policy that is clear and fully supported.

- o Find out if your target companies have a preferred area of sponsorship – for example the arts, sport or charity.
- o Do they have strong philosophical or social standpoints?
- o Does your policy align or clash with these standpoints?

SPONSORSHIP HIGHLIGHT 3.1

How sponsorship deals benefit large companies
5 MAY 2012, *Written by Farzana Baduel,*

Source:
http://www.businessrevieweurope.eu/marketing/mobile-marketing/how-sponsorship-deals-benefit-large-companies

Sponsorship is an avenue of marketing that can have many benefits, as long as the events or products sponsored are correctly targeted and relevant to the objectives the company wants to achieve.

Sponsoring gives large companies an opportunity to be seen by their clients, employees and stakeholders to support another brand that holds desired values and prestige. They can thus take advantage of the 'reflected glory' that association with a bigger and possibly more established brand can bring.

Sponsoring enables large companies to focus on specific sections of their target audience, such as ethnic minorities (sponsoring an ethnic minority event) or sports lovers (sponsoring a game) and therefore resonates more strongly with niche audiences than a mass promotion and in today's world, reaching a target audience and showing your customers that you are interested in them is incredibly important. Sponsoring not for profit or charities also sends positive CSR messages about the large companies. As consumer decisions are increasingly influenced by the extent of corporations CSR agenda, this is becoming a more pertinent factor in sponsorship decisions. This is also a great way to gain additional marketing collateral, as the wider consumer press tends to cover charity and sporting events much more readily than corporate ones.

Large companies can also garner support in its immediate operating area or distribution points by sponsoring local community projects. While this is also important for local businesses, even large multinational corporations have acknowledged the great benefit to be gained from establishing an interest in small local communities, as a vehicle for representing themselves in the light of a 'company that cares' at a local level. Sponsoring also can bring a 'cool factor' to a company's brand by choosing fashion, art, music, racing events, brands to sponsor, take a look at the likes of Red Bull and Virgin who have achieved great success by sponsoring events.

Companies that may be completely un-associated with art for example, like a bank, will choose to establish an interest via sponsorship, in order to give themselves a 'luxury' or 'intellectual' or 'cultural' profile in the minds of their high-end customers. It can thus serve as a complimentary component of branding.

Sponsoring not only allows the company to communicate to its sponsorship to its employees, customers, stake-holders but also to the wider audience it is accessing via sponsorship. By associating itself with and event or brand it will indirectly be accessing the database and extending its reach beyond its typical or traditional sphere of influence.

Other than having its brand on marketing materials, large companies often, via sponsorship buy access to events or special seating areas, tickets, private dinners etcetera that bring kudos when they invite their key clients and employees to attend. Sponsors are often given priority at events in terms of table, seat or box allocation and this can be key in networking at the event, as well as giving them added prestige among VIP clients invited to take advantage of their access to the event.

Sponsoring a specific area such as art sends a message to its target audience (art lovers) that the company is 'my kind of people' and therefore that their values are in sync, for example Deutche Bank sponsors the Frieze Contemporary Art Fair, in Regents Park, London each year, and in turn the bank is therefore able to give their clients and key staff special access to the fair.

Sponsoring of historic events such as the Olympics, gives corporations the opportunity to participate in something with great historic significance. This is a massive press opportunity as coverage will be worldwide and comprehensive. It gives companies unparalleled access to markets across the globe, and at the same time associates them with the 'best in the world' calibre of participants. Sponsoring individual teams can also bring the added benefit of being seen as supporting their home country and building a strong profile as for example, British company, Lloyd's TSB sponsoring the 2102 London Games.

In the short term benefits accruing from sponsorship are largely that such associations promote the company brand to a new audience through exposure of 'sponsor logos'.

In the long term benefits can include helping to build relationships when clients and employees are invited as guests to sponsored events.

It further builds trust in clients and employees that the company is supporting 'good causes'. Moreover the subliminal effects of repeated exposure to logos in association with prestigious social, cultural, sporting and charitable events is well documented, hence the corporate sponsorship of Formula 1 racing. One study showed that the most common brand often associated with Formula 1 racing, in the minds of spectators, was Pirelli Tires, which has never sponsored a car, but has always had their banner most prominently and strategically displayed over the race-track.

Long-term collaborations resulting from sponsorship, such as Pirelli and Formula 1, can build a company image for years to come in the minds of the public and help a brand to align itself with within a particular sector that may be outside its direct traditional domain. They can also help off-set a negative image that the company has been struggling with, so for example, McDonalds has recently launched an 'Olympic Plan to get Kids moving'. In addition as a top-tier International Olympic Committee sponsor, McDonald's will provide the only branded food in the Olympic Park and the Athlete's Village, including its largest restaurant in the world; all this to dispel its image as a purveyor of unhealthy food. So it stands to reason that sponsorship works and is an invaluable marketing tool.

FURTHER READING

Sponsorship: A Case Study, *HQ Research*,
http://www.iapco.org/wp-content/uploads/2013/08/Sponsorship-a-Case-Study.pdf

LaFleur, A., (2012), Sponsorships: Who should we start targeting?, *Esports Business*, May 8,
http://esportsbusiness.com/sponsorships-who-should-we-start-targeting/

FROM THE EXPERTS

- ❖ 'I want you understand my company, our marketing campaigns, our goals, our visions. You can learn this in your initial conversation with your prospective sponsor or on social media or on our sponsor's web site.'
- ❖ 'Your goal is not to get me to say "yes" over the phone, your goal is to arrange a personal meeting with me.'
- ❖ 'Do not take the word 'no' as a rejection. Take it as a request for more and/or better information.'

SPONSORSHIP FACT:

Latin American consumers are most trusting of brand sponsorships, with 81 percent of both Colombians and Venezuelans, and 79 percent of Brazilians, trusting brand sponsorships.

U.S. consumers came in 12th, with 72 percent trusting brand sponsorships. Sponsorships held the least sway among Swedes (33 percent), Latvians (36 percent) and Finns (38 percent).

Four

Discovering your target's sponsorship policy

'Nothing is more expensive than missed opportunity.'
H. JACKSON BROWN

Having identified the organisations with the most potential for mutual satisfaction, the next step is to find out about their sponsorship policy. Just as *you* have precluded making an agreement with certain companies (your 'no-go' areas), *they* may have a company sponsorship policy that locks you out of their consideration.

Your property might appeal to a range of sponsors, but you need to know which companies are most likely to take you on. Most sponsors have a fairly clear idea of who or what they will sponsor. For instance, it would take some very well-constructed arguments for you to convince a sponsor with a policy of dealing exclusively with the arts to sponsor your rugby team. Of course, there can be quite idiosyncratic reasons why a company will choose one property over another, and sometimes the decision will rest on something as simple as the whim or interests of the managing director. What chance will a dance company who targets an insurance company have if the managing director of that company is a horse-racing fanatic and will not allow the company to sponsor anything else? If your matching process reveals a solid, well-established barrier, don't waste your time and energy.

To increase the probability of success, you will have to do some homework. You need to know about potential sponsors' policies, and in some detail. I have encountered far too many event managers who came to the table with no real knowledge of my company, its policies or its personnel. They came armed with two pieces of information only: that we used sponsorship as a marketing tool and that our sponsorship portfolio included properties from their event category. They used my relatively rare and precious time to fact-find. Often the meeting was a waste of everyone's time, and successful conclusions for all were seldom reached.

There were times, for example, when an enthusiastic delegation would arrive brandishing a cannot-fail, bound-to-impress proposal destined to make all parties deliriously happy. They would regale me with facts and figures, show me beautifully prepared graphs and sing a siren song of soaring profits for all concerned. Eventually they would reveal that they were requesting sponsorship for an under-age event. Of course, ethically, legally and morally, such events cannot be associated with alcohol. The community would be outraged, our company image would take a beating and in all probability, I would have lost my job. In these cases, the simplest research would have saved much time and aggravation.

Happily, there were plenty of well-prepared and well-informed individuals too; who arrived at meetings armed with facts and knowledge enough to enter fruitful negotiations.

How to research your target's sponsorship policy

Utilise an inside contact

Let's not be coy – we live in a 'who you know' world, and it's far easier to glean information from friends, colleagues and networking than from people you don't know. An inside contact is an extremely important source of information. They work for the company, know who the relevant people are and may be aware of the company's sponsorship policies, even if only in broad terms. On the face of it, this would seem a strange decision. Here was readily available money – money for which they had had to expend no effort, and yet they knocked us back. I respected the decision, however, which was based on a strict association policy: no sponsorship deals with cigarette or alcohol companies. They had a well thought-out policy and stuck by it.

You should do likewise. Have a list of target sponsors (as discussed earlier), but also decide where you will draw the line and which companies or products lie beyond that line. There was once a media circus that developed when, in Melbourne, Australia, a suburban, non professional football club accepted a sponsorship offer from a local legal brothel. News footage showed the establishment's workers cheering lustily from the sidelines, backing their 'property' – the local football champions – to the hilt. While the story generated considerable amusement for some and righteous indignation for others, many of those closely associated with the club, including the players' partners, were clearly unconvinced of the sponsorship 'fit'.

Would such an arrangement accord with your organisation's aims? What would be your reaction if a controversial firm offered you a lucrative deal? Would you accept an offer from a company known to be affecting the environment adversely through its business activities? Would you accept a deal from an organization that is involved in the killing and harvesting of whales? How would you handle the internal conflict if some of your members or personnel insisted on taking the deal while others refused? Every scout knows the answer: be prepared. If you have never sat down and clearly defined your philosophical and ethical perspective, look at the research exercise at the end of this chapter and do it now.

This may exclude some of your intended target sponsors. The important thing is never to be discouraged. If the companies on your first list are not the right fit for your organisation and its goals, keep going. In the words of inventor Alexander Graham Bell, 'When one door closes, another opens; but we so often look so long and so regretfully at the closed door, that we do not see the ones which open for us.'

Choosing the right sponsor

When starting the search for a sponsor, you should first identify the product categories and segments that target consumers with similar needs to those attracted to or involved in your property. Various groups and bodies offer support packages, so don't limit your search to a narrow band of targets. When making your list of potential backers, consider:
- large, multinational corporations
- national firms of all sizes
- state-based firms and companies of all sizes
- federal and state governments
- local councils
- neighbourhood businesses of all sizes
- Philanthropic trusts or individuals.

To decide which segments will present you with the best chance of success, look critically at both what you have to offer and what you need. For example, the requirements of a small community-based hockey club or a local charity fundraising group will probably be nicely met by the local traders – a car dealership, a flower shop, the corner convenience store or a pizza restaurant. A more professional and higher-profile hockey team playing in a regional competition may need more funds to remain competitive, but can offer a potential sponsor greater exposure. Such a club should seek dollar support from medium to large companies.

A concern that is bigger still, for example a hockey team that plays in national or international competition, or a large charity organisation like the Red Cross, would be well advised to approach a major national or multi-national corporation. Cultural or artistic groups should consider casting their net in the direction of various government bodies, philanthropists, sympathetic trusts or businesses that have already demonstrated an interest in using the arts as a marketing vehicle. Don't be afraid to raise your sights. If you have traditionally targeted local small businesses, why not try a handful of larger organisations? It is probably more important that your organisation matches their strategic need and philosophical outlook than their size.

Ask your contact detailed questions that cover every angle, right down to which football team the sponsorship Manager supports. Such information may be of value as an icebreaker if you gain a meeting with this person. If you can build a rapport with them simply by generating a conversation about how their team played last Saturday, how much could you achieve with more information?

The session with your insider is not a time for you to talk or direct the conversation. If you add too many of your own ideas and opinions, you risk colouring your contact's thought processes when what you hope to achieve is undistorted information direct from their memory. Certainly you can and should use prompting techniques, asking 'how' and 'why', but above all listen keenly and record every detail.

The Greek philosopher Epictetus once said, 'We have two ears and one mouth so that we can listen twice as much as we speak.'

Heed his advice.

Call the company

You may not have the luxury of an insider. What then? If you are just looking for basic information such as names, titles and their correct address, by all means call the company. You will probably be transferred to the departmental secretary, who is a significant figure in the organisation and should be treated with due deference. Never make the tactical error of treating them like a lackey. Everyone in that company is worthy of respect and this person wields considerable power. Should you create an unfavourable impression, you will be stonewalled despite your best efforts.

Conversely, if you are overly familiar your cause may be harmed even more. These are intelligent, capable and experienced people who are not going to fall for sycophantic, effusive nonsense.

Be genuine. Play it straight with them and treat them with respect – they can become your ally, helping to smooth your path into the inner sanctum.

You could approach your target directly for more detailed information, but this is not a course of action I would recommend. From my experience, most sponsorship managers are reluctant to release detailed information either because they have no time or because they are careful not to divulge too much that might be considered confidential.

Make use of public information

The daily newspapers and business magazines are awash with pertinent information. They will often have general reports on a company's involvement in the arts or its charitable works, or carry stories and photographs of sponsorship signings. Graze for information, asking who is sponsoring what and whether yours is an area in which they might be looking to expand.

The financial pages provide insights into the fiscal state of companies and corporations. If a target company has performed poorly and announced a profit loss, they are more likely to be jettisoning existing properties than taking on new ones. Where healthy profit increases lie, there also lies opportunity.

Other research material might include annual reports, specialist publications, trade magazines, radio, television and the Internet. One often-neglected source of material is the Yellow Pages telephone directory, where all classifications of businesses are presented in easily accessible, alphabetical lists. Although in the advent of the internet, it is still a very useful tool. It may seem arcane to suggest Yellow Pages directories, and one that gives away my age. However, you need to utilise every tool at your disposal in the quest for sponsors. And further, don't knock it until you try it.

By these means you can build a profile of the companies you are investigating, compare and contrast their feasibility, and discover who is sponsoring what and for how much, all while whittling your list down to a shining few.

The power and pull of social media

The first modern social media tool was, arguably, the humble telephone followed by the fax machine and then email. Today we have Facebook, LinkedIn, Tumblr, Twitter, YouTube, Skype and a host of other social media platforms whose numbers seem to multiply on a daily basis. The rapid adoption of social interaction through these platforms has allowed something that started as a fad to develop into a trend and then break through as a fully integrated and legitimate tool for doing business.

As an example, the extraordinary effect Twitter and Skype had on the Red-Cross fundraising and recovery efforts during and after the 2010 Haiti earthquake had a dramatic and long term effect on disaster management and not-for-profit fundraising. Both social media provided situational information, reported on food and aid availability, locations of safe havens and shelters and movements of people. They also reported on road closures and diversions and where locations where mobile phones could be recharged.

Social media allows for organisations to track and follow potential sponsors. From clicking "likes" on face book to gain current updates on prospects, to examining prospects' profiles on LinkedIn and Twitter to identify their job roles and to get a feel for them as people not just a name.

The information you need to obtain

Using the methods suggested above as appropriate, find out for each of your potential sponsor companies:
   ❖ how and why they use sponsorship as a marketing tool
   ❖ the composition of their sponsorship portfolio – the types and categories of events, individuals or
   ❖ organisations they support
   ❖ whether they have any policy that effectively bars them from supporting your venture
   ❖ what level of spend, in ballpark figures, do they allocate to sponsorship per annum
   ❖ what, in ballpark figures, they allocate to individual properties.

A number of previously promising targets will drop off the list at this stage. Identifying impediments early in your endeavours saves time, effort and, often, face. When you are ill informed and ill prepared you send a negative message to a company. You are dealing with professionals, so don't look like an amateur!

LESSONS TO TAKE FROM THIS CHAPTER

- ❖ Do the spadework. Research your targets and refine your list of potential sponsors.
- ❖ Consult your contacts to glean some finer detail.
- ❖ The more information you have, the better prepared you will be.

SUGGESTED RESEARCH EXERCISE

To hone your listening techniques:

1. Find a friend or acquaintance who works for a company known to use sponsorship as a marketing tool. (The company does not need to be a potential target – this is just an exercise.) Ask your friend to tell you all they know about the company's involvement in sponsorship. After an initial briefing in which you will explain what you are trying to do, sit back and allow your friend to speak freely. Only interrupt when absolutely necessary, to ask probing questions or to seek clarification.

2. How much information did you receive? Did it provide you with a clear insight into the company's stance on sponsorship? Do you now know enough about the company to make a sound judgement about whether they would be interested in your property or whether you are interested in them? Have you placed this company in the 'hot prospect' or 'non-starter' category as a result of this exercise?

3. Tell your friend everything you learned from their talk. Then ask whether you gave them a true account of all they said. Did you miss or misinterpret any salient points? Did you add anything your friend did not mention because you took it for granted?

FROM THE EXPERTS

- ❖ 'Economic times are tough; everyone is vying for the same corporate dollars and the pickings even slimmer. But anyone can enhance their chances of success by understanding the needs of the sponsor.'

❖ 'Exhaustively research companies with a strong presence within your community and identify those with a commitment to your organisation's cause.'

MANDATORY REQUIREMENTS FROM THE EXPERTS

The following is a list of what the experts say must be provided to them to ensure that your application will be considered:
❖ A list of the key values of your organisation.
❖ Identification of your target market/audience is. Can you accurately and adequately describe them?
❖ How do you plan to advertise and promote your event/program? Can you guarantee my company and brands exposure?
❖ We demand cconfirmation that we will be the only company within our industry segment allied with your organisation/event/program. Can you guarantee exclusivity to me?
❖ A full list of your current or previous supporters (if any).
❖ Your contact details in full.

LISTENING SKILLS

TRY THIS	AVOID THIS
Dedicate specific time to work on listening skills	Promising to work on your skills throughout the day when you never actually get time to do it
Minimise how much you talk and limit interruptions & distractions	Dominating the conversation, taking the lead by suggesting topics, asking questions, offering advice, derailing the speaker's train of thought or multi-tasking during the conversation
Concentrate on the intended message	Identifying episodes of stuttering or judging effectiveness purely on fluency level
Be open to a variety of topics generated by the speaker	Only discuss topic that are interesting to you or attempt to steer the conversation
Be aware of your eye contact, body language and body proximity	Make listening an after thought or attempt to listen while doing something else

Be conscious of the feelings associated with the message	Assuming feelings, minimising actual feelings or placating emotions (yeah, yeah; I see)

FURTHER CHECKLIST OF INFORMATION THE POTENTIAL SPONSOR WILL WANT FROM YOU

- ❖ Can you and have you provided a full list of sponsorship benefits?
- ❖ What are the dates and location of the sponsorship? Do these dates clash with anything else I am involved in?
- ❖ Is the activity a one off event or does it reoccur annually?
- ❖ Can our employees be involved, and if so how?
- ❖ Is there any hospitality, entertainment or general involvement for our customers to participate in?
- ❖ Is there any current or potential business the organisation does or can do with us?
- ❖ Which media partners have been confirmed and what will be the media exposure?
- ❖ Will there be national exposure for your event or activity?
- ❖ Does your organisation/event compliment our existing sponsor partnerships?

- ❖ What is the reach of the sponsorship?
- ❖ How many people see, attend or are involved?
- ❖ What is the maximum number of sponsors who could be involved and what are the levels / hierarchy?
- ❖ Has any research been undertaken to help define the target market and/or the acceptance of sponsors?
- ❖ What is the proposed cost of the proposal and what is your expected payment schedule?
- ❖ How will you measure the success or otherwise of your event and by what date and in what format will you report back to us?
- ❖ What will the funds provided by my company predominantly be used for?
- ❖ How long has the organisation been in operation, what is its history and long-term goals?
- ❖ How will the organisation manage the partnership, will there be an account manager?

SPONSORSHIP FACT

Beer brands are the most active category in the area of sponsorship in Ireland. H however beer consumption in Ireland has been in significant decline in recent years.

RESEARCH SKILLS
Source: http://www.maggiehosmcgrane.com/2012_11_01_archive.html

Research skills	
Formulating questions	Identifying something one wants or needs to know and asking compelling and relevant questions that can be researched.
Observing	Using all the senses to notice relevant details.
Planning	Developing a course of action; writing an outline; devising ways of finding out necessary information.
Collecting data	Gathering information from a variety of first- and second-hand sources such as maps, surveys, direct observation, books, films, people, museums and ICT.
Recording data	Describing and recording observations by drawing, note taking, making charts, tallying, writing statements.
Organizing data	Sorting and categorizing information; arranging into understandable forms such as narrative descriptions, tables, timelines, graphs and diagrams.
Interpreting data	Drawing conclusions from relationships and patterns that emerge from organized data.
Presenting research findings	Effectively communicating what has been learned; choosing appropriate media.

Five

Auditing your marketable assets

'Opportunities multiply as they are seized.'
Sun Tzu

This chapter plots the point where you stop briefly from your anxious rush into the maze and spend some time looking internally to gauge your strengths and learn about your organization to evaluate its worth relative to sponsors' expectations. I once attended a seminar on obtaining sponsorship, where a variety of associations gathered to uncover sponsorship secrets from eminently qualified experts. The seminar was a two-day affair with much useful and relevant information disseminated, but I went away feeling that a lot of important information had not been covered. The missing component, by my reckoning, related to what the associations had to offer a prospective sponsor.

The matter could have been framed in two questions:
  ❖ What value do you place on your organisation?
  ❖ What are your organisation's saleable assets?

Interestingly, many of the presenters had bemoaned the lack of anything worthwhile to offer potential sponsors, but had overcome that considerable hurdle by devising ingenious strategies to promote their organisation. For example, a senior marketing executive from a high-profile sporting body told the assembly that all her organisation had to hang its hat on was a major annual one-day event, even though the club held events throughout the year. Her message was that without that major event, her club would have little to attract sponsors.

Don't be like this person, taking a narrow view of the market and underestimating your own organisation's offerings. You don't find gold nuggets lying about in the streets; you have to work extremely hard to find a speck here and a pebble there. Whether your organisation is small or large is not an issue – it is imperative that you start digging. And dig with a fresh perspective, one that re-evaluates and redefines. While it is true to say that upon major events hinge all other activities of a club, I would expect any organisation facing a similar situation to consider the two questions missing from the seminar.

An audit is invaluable. This is an empowering process that enables you to package your organisation attractively and effectively to the sponsors you approach. Set out to map all your saleable assets – you are bound to unearth a number of opportunities of value and benefit to prospective targets.

Stage 1: Identify your marketable assets

An assets audit is vital to any organisation if it is to run smoothly and efficiently. Not an audit that counts the dollars in the bank or the number of chairs, tables and items of equipment stacked in your storeroom, but an audit of events or properties that will appeal to a sponsor. Such an audit should be part of your business plan. To develop a suitable plan, you must understand your organisation and its market. Why? Because you will have a much better grasp of your offerings and their worth to you and, more importantly, to your target sponsors. The list you compile should catalogue everything you have. A detailed assets analysis such as this, done with saleability in mind, forces you to evaluate and more fully appreciate your properties. It may even inspire some new way of looking at an old property that you have failed to fully exploit. Suddenly you realize that you have more than you thought.

So what are your marketable assets? You have probably already started to mentally list those applying to your organisation, but for the sake of this exercise, let's look at a medium-sized sporting club involved in team sports – I'll call it the Leopards. It will most likely have:
- ❖ Clubrooms
- ❖ a couple of playing fields, with perimeter fencing around each
- ❖ team uniforms
- ❖ a weekly newsletter
- ❖ hot and cold food and snack sales
- ❖ a licensed bar
- ❖ lots of supporters
- ❖ various annual functions including a club dinner dance, an awards night, an auction and a trivia night
- ❖ players and members.

How assets might be used

You may be able to add even more items, but for the moment, let's consider what the Leopards have that might entice sponsorship. Every asset can be attractive to a potential sponsor. Think about how a sponsor might be able to use these assets. The intrepid Leopards could sell:

- ❖ naming rights to their clubrooms, for example, the Toyota Pavilion
- ❖ signs on the internal and/or external walls of the clubrooms
- ❖ naming rights for both the playing fields (it has been done before and can be done again, as highlighted in Chapter one)
- ❖ advertising space on the perimeter fences
- ❖ sponsor logos on all team jumpers, track suits and playing shorts
- ❖ advertising in the newsletter (possibly up to 1000 copies distributed weekly)
- ❖ product categories that could be converted into exclusive product sales rights for the sponsor, for example:
  - beer
  - soft drink
  - pies, pasties, pastries and doughnuts, french fries
  - snack foods
  - the database of club members (this mailing list can be used by the sponsor to communicate directly with club supporters so long as the supporters have consented to the release of their details for the purpose of direct marketing)
  - naming rights to all functions and events; for example, Budweiser Lightning Premiership, Leopards Black Tie Ball sponsored by Yoplait
  - sponsorship of individual A-grade players by companies or individuals (this has been done successfully by many clubs, with the sponsored player's photograph displayed in the clubrooms and the sponsor's name positioned prominently beneath it).

So without working too hard, we have identified several genuinely sponsorable assets that will be of serious interest to a target sponsor – things that would add weight to any proposal. The Leopards, it seems, in the ordinary conduct of their core business, are already a viable proposition for sponsorship. Is your organisation?

Think in terms of what you have that a sponsor would be willing to pay for.

A checklist of ideas for inclusion

This analytical approach applies to all types of organisations. If you undertake an assets audit, you will surely produce a list of benefits that you can bundle into an attractive and saleable package.

Concrete items

List the physical assets you may be able to use to benefit a sponsor. This could include clubrooms, playing fields, perimeter fencing and team uniforms, as in the case of the Leopards, which can be used to display sponsor messages. Use the example above and think laterally – arts organisations might display sponsor logos on theatre seating or, for a gallery display, on the exhibits' explanatory labels.

Events

List the annual events run by your organisation and ask:
❖ Are any of these events significant enough to catch the attention of a sponsor?
❖ Can we revamp any of our existing events in terms of size, timing or community involvement so that they are better tailored to attract sponsors?
❖ Can we create any new events or occasions that will attract sponsors to our organisation?
❖ Can we change the name of any of our events to give them more appeal?
❖ Can we offer event naming rights?

The organisation itself

❖ Do we have any high-profile members who may be willing to become part of the enticement to target sponsors?
❖ Has our organisation had any recent success with which prospective sponsors might want to align themselves?
❖ Do our members fall into a certain demographic that invites specific targeting? (For example, a cricket club might well attract an alcohol company/bottle shop or a sportswear manufacturer, whereas a scout group or four-wheel drive club may appeal to a manufacturer of products for the great outdoors.)

Signage and other advertising opportunities

❖ Does our organisation border any carriageways (the busier the better) where signs can face passing traffic and be read daily by passing potential consumers?
❖ Can sponsors' messages be permanently attached to perimeter fences or in the clubrooms?

❖ Can sponsor logos be placed on all stationery and mail-outs?
❖ Can sponsors' advertising material or promotional offers be included in all mail-outs?

Supporters and members

❖ Would our members be willing for us to provide a sponsor with the membership list for direct mailing purposes? (Note that you must obtain your members' consent because of laws protecting the privacy of personal information.)
❖ Are we able to offer sampling opportunities for our sponsor's products and services?
❖ Would our members and supporters be willing to cooperate with market research?

Product usage

❖ Can we assure a sponsor that we will continually encourage members to support them by purchasing their products and services.
❖ Can we detail our strategy and/or produce evidence of our efforts?
  o You can do this by constantly reinforcing a simple message to members: support the sponsor and the sponsor will continue to support our organisation.
  o Members can be encouraged to tell the sponsor which organisation they support, giving the sponsor first-hand evidence of sales being directly attributable to sponsorship support.
  o You can also ask your members to provide you with receipts after purchasing sponsor products.
  o A robust pile of receipts can be pleasant and convincing evidence of support to even the most skeptical of sponsors.
❖ Can we identify the number of members a sponsor will reach as a result of our partnership, thereby demonstrating the number of potential new users of the sponsor's product?

Existing sponsors

❖ Do we have existing sponsors whose support demonstrates to others that our organisation is a safe and reliable investment? (Often events boasting high-profile sponsors will more easily attract other sponsors who realise that high-profile sponsors have already thoroughly evaluated the benefits.
  o I was often approached to supply no more than my

company's advertising material – no money, no products, just a presence. The idea was that if a sponsor of the size and reputation of my company had faith in the organisation, it must be worthwhile.)

Power-boosted bait

Some organisations will have another powerfully baited hook at their disposal, one with the potential to increase their assets' sponsorship value. That hook is the media. If you are willing to purchase advertising or can obtain a sponsorship deal with a newspaper, television network or radio station, or a combination, the net effect is that you now have something very attractive with which to dress up your proposal: you can offer free media exposure to sponsors who come on board. Remember the earlier exercise when I asked you to peruse newspaper advertisements and photos and see just how many sponsor logos appeared, apparently incidentally, in prominent positions? This kind of media exposure opportunity is an almost irresistible hook for your target fish.

The above are simply ideas to whet your appetite and to get your creative juices flowing. You know your own organization better than anyone. With careful thought and some imagination, inspiration and resourcefulness you will develop and craft your own long list of marketable assets.

Stage 2: Identify factors affecting your organisation

This stage seeks to determine:
❖ the size of the market in which you operate
❖ the type and density of competition
❖ the trends that have an impact on your property.

You should conduct an internal and external analysis of the type used widely in various disciplines and often referred to as a SWOT analysis (see Figure 4). Internally it looks at strengths and weaknesses within the organisation. These are factors over which you have control and can therefore modify as required. The analysis of external opportunities and threats examines factors over which you have little control but which you may accommodate by making adjustments or contingency plans. A SWOT analysis will produce a picture of where your organization stands in relation to all the factors that will have an impact on it. It is a 'big picture' snapshot that will help you to make market-canny decisions.

Strengths

Ascertain what your organisation is good at, what it does best and how these strengths can be used to its best advantage.

Weaknesses

Identify weaknesses. Are there gaps in your skills that hinder your ability to perform at maximum effectiveness?

Opportunities

Identify any changes in the market that might yield opportunities. These are external influences that can significantly benefit your organisation even though they are largely beyond your control. (One example was the 'millennium bug' phenomenon. Globally, companies spent over $100 billion to go through their entire application source codes to look for the Y2K bug and fix it. An estimated $12 billion was spent in Australia alone to ensure that the impact of Y2K was negated or minimal, which was a windfall to those companies involved in providing solutions to the problem.)

Threats

Identify any variables such as changes in economic forces or new competition that might frustrate your cause. (For example, who could have foreseen the enormous shortfall on available sponsorship funds that the 2000 Sydney Olympics had on Australian sponsorship seekers for at least two years after the event?)

For some organisations the SWOT analysis will appear to produce a long list of strengths and one or two weaknesses. This is a time of complete honesty. Do it again, this time digging deeper and, no matter how much internal conflict may be tossed up, continue until you have a complete list. Then follow Figure 4. It is designed to help you to establish objectives for your organisation.

Stage 3: Make your assets into packages

Now that you have conducted both an internal and an external assets audit, the next step is to decide how much you are going to ask from sponsors. To do this, you need to bundle the marketable assets identified into packages and then cost them, taking into account their attractiveness to sponsors, and ensuring that they will receive value for the proposed fee.

Figure 4: SWOT Analysis

HOW CAN WE BUILD ON OUR STRENGTHS?	HOW TO OVERCOME OUR WEAKNESSES?
List all the resources that we can muster and apply to increase our strengths. - Value to sponsors - Competitive advantage - Capabilities - Unique Selling Proposition (USP) - Resources, assets, people, experience, knowledge - Marketing – reach, distribution, awareness - Location - Price, quality, exclusivity - Accreditations, qualifications, certifications	List all the methods at our disposal that we can utilise to reduce these weaknesses - No perceived value by sponsors - Gaps in capabilities - Lack of a competitive advantage - Similarity of our event to like events - Lack of reputation or profile - Time pressures and looming deadlines - Morale, commitment, leadership
HOW CAN WE TAKE ADVANTAGE OF ANY OPPORTUNITIES? What benefits would we receive by expending effort and resources to pursue these opportunities? - Market developments - Competing events/activities become vulnerable - Changing lifestyles and trends - Innovation development - Global influences - Strategic alliances	**HOW CAN WE MINIMISE ANY THREATS?** What steps can we take and what would it cost to reduce the effects of the external environment on our plans? - Political/legal changes - Decreasing market demand - Competitor aggression - Loss of key staff - Insurmountable obstacles

Bundling up your assets

Consider how you can bundle all of the items that have been identified in order to attract sponsors. Here are a few suggestions on how to mix and match items so that as a bundle or package they provide greater value than they would individually:

1. Naming rights to the club's playing field (for example, Singapore Airlines or Nescafe or Duracell Oval), plus strategic signage on the perimeter fence (viewed by patrons), plus signage facing out towards the streets for maximum reach (viewed by passing motorists and pedestrians).

2. Naming rights to the club (Kellogg's or Gillette or Ikea Leopards), plus strategic signage on the ground perimeter fence and club buildings, plus outward-facing signage, plus logos on player uniforms and training clothing, plus major product advertising in club publications, plus exclusive product sales and usage at the club, plus a hospitality package.

3. Naming rights to the club bar (Bitburger or Coors or Tiger Bar), plus exclusive beer rights to Bitburger/Coors/Tiger within the club at all home games and at all functions, plus signage. These bundled offerings are now attractive as they contain several distinct opportunities that may fit the overall strategic requirements of sponsors. Draw up a document like that in Figure 5. Then estimate the value of your offerings to determine the fee you will ask for each package.

Figure 5: The Leopards' sponsorship packages.

	MAJOR	GOLD	SILVER	BRONZE	SUPPORT
Number	One only	3 only	5 only	8 only	Up to 15
Amount	$10,000	$5,000	$1,000	$500	$150
Level	Naming rights	Associate Second tier	Adjunct Third tier	Allied Fourth tier	Support Fifth tier
Advertising	Premium	'AA' level	'B' level	'C' level	'D' level
Seating	VIP x 10	Prime x 6	'B' x 6	'B' x 4	'B' x 2
Hospitality	10 Prime	Prime x 6	'B' x 6	'B' x 4	N/a
Signage	'AAA'	'AA' level	'B' level	'C' level	'D' level

LESSONS TO TAKE FROM THIS CHAPTER

- ❖ Preparation and analysis are vital.
- ❖ List all the products you sell or use and use this list to identify potential sponsors.
- ❖ Plot your assets – inanimate and human.
- ❖ Determine how each asset can be used by sponsors.

- ❖ Consider your capacity to sweeten the deal with media exposure.
- ❖ Conduct a SWOT analysis.
- ❖ Know your market value relative to like competition.

SUGGESTED RESEARCH EXERCISE

Imagine that you are to leave your home to relocate in some far-off and exotic country. You can't take anything with you except your clothing and your most valued possessions, so you are going to conduct a garage sale. Make up two lists. On one list, write down all of your items that could be readily sold. On the other, list all of those 'junk' items that would most likely end up in the local rubbish dump.

Your task is to sell every item listed – the ones on the 'good' list as well as those on the 'junk' list. Be as creative as possible in determining what benefits the 'junk' items might deliver to prospective purchasers and develop pitches that have the power to sell them. You can bundle several items to make them more appealing to buyers. The object of this exercise is to highlight the fact that some items you consider worthless often have value to others. Garage sales prove this point. Next time you see a sign advertising a garage sale, stop and look at the items people buy. Every time I want to rid myself of unwanted items a garage sale does the job and provides me with a few extra dollars. Similarly, those items within your organisation that don't seem to have any value in your estimation often do in the eyes of others. The benefit to you is that these items can generate sponsorship

FROM THE EXPERTS

'In the world of corporate sponsorships, your demographic (also called the target audience) is one of the most valuable assets that you can offer a corporate sponsor.'

FURTHER READING

Tighe, G., From Experience: Securing Sponsors and Funding for New Product Development Projects—The Human Side of Enterprise , Journal of Product Innovation Management, *Vol. 15, Iss. 1, pages 75–81, January 1998*

http://www.entrepreneur.com/article/217913

http://www.richardwoodward.com.au/how-to-become-effective-at-securing-sponsorship/

http://theassociationspecialists.com.au/2013/08/top-5-tips-on-securing-sponsorship/

http://www.rosemariespeaks.com/meeting-planner/sponsors.cfm

SPONSORSHIP FACT

Sponsorship funding can be allocated to pay for a myriad of specific costs incurred by an event. Depending on the event, these could costs include, traffic control, emergency medical coverage, liability insurance, security, food for event participants, etc.

Six

Planning your spending spree

'Price is what you pay.
Value is what you get.'
WARREN BUFFETT

This chapter is short and to the point, but its message is extremely important. It asks you the simple question, 'Why?'

In interviews I often posed the question this way:
* ❖ 'If I agree to your request, what are you going to do with the money?'
* ❖ And I ask you now: How will you spent it ? Why do you want that amount of money?

Don't be vague. A blank look from you when the question is asked does nothing to engender faith in your proposal. The story doesn't end with your need for revenue; in fact, that is only where the dialogue starts. If you can't lay out a strategy for using the funds, the potential sponsor might wonder if, once you had the money, you might not spend it frivolously.

A strong financial plan

Before you even contemplate approaching a target, get your house in order:
* ❖ Initiate a sound fundraising policy and ensure that all relevant people in your organisation understand and accept it.
* ❖ Draw up a list, in order of importance, of all events, items and areas in which the funds will be spent.
* ❖ Cost them, and provide a cost analysis that sets out the total input required from the sponsor if such projects are to be realized (see Figure 7).

This exercise is worthwhile anyway because it helps to clarify the present and future needs of your organisation and quantifies your funding requirements. It may be that it triggers new ideas, uncovers new opportunities or reinvigorates your committee's zeal.

Figure 7: Sample budget for a medium-sized sporting club.

OPERATING COSTS FOR YEAR ENDING 31/12/XXXX $250,000
REVENUES FROM CLUB FUNDRAISING $150,000
TOTAL SHORTFALL (SPONSORSHIP REQUIRED) $100,000

SHORTFALL ALLOCATED TO:

ITEM	BUDGET
Uniforms	$5,000
Training equipment	$10,000
Clubhouse renovations	$25,000
Medical supplies	$5,000
Travel expenses	$10,000
Coaching staff payments	$20,000
Administration overheads	$10,000
Player insurance	$5,000
Ground/arena maintenance	$10,000
BUDGET SHORTFALL	**$100 000**

OBJECTIVE OF THE ABOVE BUDGET: To match sponsors to areas of required budget spending.

For example:

ITEM	BUDGET	TARGET
Uniforms	$5,000	Cover Me Co.
Training equipment	$10,000	XL Sports Store
Clubhouse renovations	$25,000	Para Paint Co.
Medical supplies	$5,000	Tom's Pharma
Travel expenses	$10,000	Bill's Bus Co.
Coaching staff payments	$20,000	Lazy B Hotel
Administration overheads	$10,000	BB Financial
Player insurance	$5,000	Gotcha Covered
Ground/arena maintenance	$10,000	LL Seed Supply
BUDGET SHORTFALL	**$100 000**	

Also ensure that your financial management is sound. Sponsors get a little edgy when they see that a potential property has finished the year in the red or with an embarrassing surplus. It indicates poor planning, financial mismanagement or a general lack of direction, when what they want to see is evidence that their funds are in safe hands and will be used judiciously.

What difference will the money make?

Sponsors' investments may well fill a gaping void between the total funds you can raise internally and the total running costs of your organisation or event. In terms of total revenue received, sponsorship funding often contributes a significant proportion, but it should never be assigned to the general financial pool. Sponsors want to see their money at work. The sponsorship must have profile.

Establish a correlation between your plans and the sponsor's input and you establish yourself as a genuine contender for the funding you seek. Be prepared to state confidently that you need new sets for your next production, commemorative buttons to sell on your next fundraising drive, or new clubrooms.

I recall negotiating an agreement with the Victorian Surf Life Saving Association. The general manager, Nigel Taylor, told me early in our discussions that part of my company's cash injection would be used to offset event costs and the remainder would be used to cover ongoing running costs. Much thought had gone into where the money would work hardest. At the trickiest phase of negotiations he presented me with figures that placed the money against specific items. He had a strategy he could confidently submit to his targets for their scrutiny. Nigel got what he came for.

What tangible outcomes can you point to: new clothing and outfits for your players? A new dance studio? attractive prize money for a race? What is your plan? Can you explain your strategies to ensure efficient and how you will maximise the use of these funds?

Clarifying the role of the sponsor

Have a well-constructed plan in which the sponsorship manager will be able to see their organisation's role clearly. Detail how their investment will help both of you achieve your goals. Outline other methods you use for fundraising and demonstrate how the sponsor's input will dovetail with these.

Target sponsors will appreciate the thoroughness and professionalism of your proposal and this will be reflected in their attitude to it. If you are well organised and can anticipate their needs, they will be far happier extending the relationship than they would be if you made them coax information out of you or, even worse, if it is not even there to be coaxed. They will rightly wonder what you will be like to work with on a continuing basis if you are like this when trying to impress.

The impact of Taxation

The importance of constantly monitoring your external environment (that is, those areas of opportunity and/or threat over which you have no control) has become even greater where there are goods and services taxes. The Goods and Services Tax (GST) and the Value-added tax (VAT) that exist in a number of countries are in essence the same. The international experience with this type of tax in countries such as New Zealand, Canada, Ireland and the United Kingdom has suggested that the implications are particularly perplexing for non-profit organisations. Although a GST has a major effect on the sponsorship industry, it may well be that it is in the arts where the greatest impact is felt. These taxes have increased admission prices in an already price-sensitive arts market: most movie, theatre, dance, live music and opera tickets have increased under this taxation system.

The arts are affected not only by cost increases through taxes on materials and subscriptions, but through the taxing of the government grants that arts organisations depend on for their survival. GST type taxes reduce the value of these grants by 10 per cent in Australia (and varies throughout the world), leaving already cash-strapped organisations with a further shortfall in resources. Sporting organisations may be in a better position than the arts in terms of sponsor attractiveness, but GSTs also impact heavily on them.

An example of the effect of GST in an Australian context is as follows:

Where an organisation receives a sponsorship of, say, $20 000, it has to invoice its benefactor a further 10 per cent ($2000) as the GST component and pay that sum as tax. Sponsors may attempt to reduce the actual sponsorship component by 10 per cent, or may build the GST into agreements. Whatever sponsors choose to do, you can be sure that they are not going to dip into their funds and willingly pay the extra without a thorough analysis of the costs and benefits.

Again it is a case of working harder and smarter. Some organisations will fall away, but the strongest and most determined will survive. In setting budgets, you need to examine, study and understand all the intricacies of GST, including the:

- ❖ total GST on all of your sponsorship income
- ❖ additional administration costs incurred by you
- ❖ impact on prices charged by your organization
- ❖ impact on sales of items at your venues.

Maybe you will uncover solutions that are to your advantage. You will need to think logically, lobby hard and argue convincingly with sponsors to gain additional funds to cover increased overheads.

LESSONS TO TAKE FROM THIS CHAPTER

- ❖ Initiate a sound fundraising policy.
- ❖ Decide where you will spend your sponsorship funds.
- ❖ Cost anything you wish to fund.
- ❖ Document the above in a financial plan and bring this plan to any meeting you have with a potential sponsor.
- ❖ Believe in your proposal.

SUGGESTED RESEARCH EXERCISES

1. What has your organisation done with funds received from sponsors in the last two years? Draw up a list of sponsors, together with their dollar input. Can you account for all these dollars, item for item? Could you honestly report back to each sponsor exactly where, when and how their support dollars were first allocated and then spent?

2. List all those areas within your organisation where sponsorship funding could be allocated, and how much each area needs. Could you justify these amounts to your sponsors?

FURTHER READING

Ferrand, (et al.), (2007), *The Routledge Handbook of Sports Sponsorship: Successful Strategies*, Routledge Press, London

Stotler, D. K., (2009), *Developing Successful Sports Sponsorship Plans* (3rd Edition), Fitness Information Technology

Kerpen, D., (2011), *Likeable Social Media: How to delight your customers, create an Irresistible brand, and be generally amazing on*

Facebook (and other social networks), McGraw-Hill, New York

Taylor, D., (2006), *Brand Vision – How to energize your team to drive business growth*, John Wiley & Sons, New York

SPONSORSHIP FACT

Sponsors are partners. They should never be treated as anything else but as a partner.

Seven

Who should enter the maze?

'History has demonstrated that the most notable winners usually encountered heartbreaking obstacles before they triumphed. They won because they refused to become discouraged by their defeats.'

B.C. FORBES

Whether you represent a junior sporting club seeking sponsors to make ends meet or pay for trophies at the end of the season, or a high-profile theatre group looking for a large sum for production expenses, you must have a professional attitude.

Who will be your representative?

Remember, sponsorship matters – and the professionalism required by those seeking it has advanced enormously in recent times. Therefore, it may be time to reconsider the representative you send into the maze. To potential sponsors, this person is the face of your organisation, so their actions, behaviour and attitudes are, to all intents and purposes, those of your organisation. But they might have been in this role for years with no one thinking to question how effective they are.

So ask yourself the following questions about your representative and consider if they the best person for the job, or are they doing it because:
- ❖ they were appointed by friends on the committee?
- ❖ no one else was willing?
- ❖ they have some influence in the organisation?

Do you know their strengths and weaknesses? (You might like to draw up a list like the one in Figure 8.)
- ❖ Have they been successful in securing significant sponsorship in the past?
- ❖ Are there people in the organisation better suited to the task than this person, by experience, business acumen or temperament?

❖ Does the person have the skill and the 'feel' necessary in the position?
❖ In other words, Do you have the best person doing this very important job?

If any of these questions make you ill at ease, it may be that you don't have the most competent person chasing your opportunities. Believe me, it is the same in large organisations as it is in small clubs – square pegs have often been jammed into round holes for so long that the imperfect fit is no longer noticed.

Let me tell you about a racehorse I once part-owned. It was an impeccably bred animal with movie-star good looks and track times to rival Black Caviar or Secretariat or the legendary Seabiscuit. A guaranteed world-beater, we thought, chuckling up our sleeves at the thought of skinning the bookies. Race days turned out rather differently. Our 'champion' was retired after posting a less than impressive 0-0-0-0. From a racing career distinguished by abject failure, he went on to become a highly successful dressage horse, now boasting many wins under his bridle. I don't need to spell it out. It's a matter of 'horses for courses' in all areas of business and life.

That's my boy...last again!!!!

But, there's my boy...first again!!!

Team players or parasites?

It's fine if you can identify the problem and find another task for this person that is more in keeping with their skills and, being good team players, they move into another area willingly. The issue becomes more complex and worrying if the incumbent is in the position because they believe that it elevates them in some way, provides them with a personal network or confers on them rank or authority. Such people are usually not so interested in or committed to your goals, except where they accord with theirs. They are not team players and can be dangerous.

How does your sponsorship representative measure up?

STRENGTHS	WEAKNESSES
- Always returns phone calls - Follows up leads and hot prospects - Has the interests of your organisation as a priority - Always does research on prospects - Is a thorough planner - Is highly motivated - Is punctual, considerate and polite - Understands your market and the needs of sponsors	- Is reluctant to follow up proposals - Takes a 'no' answer as a personal insult - Acts on their own beliefs without planning or knowledge of the market - Sees the position as an avenue to take advantage of others - Does not prioritise tasks and works in a slap-dash manner - Plays "favourites" with sponsors, under servicing some and over-servicing others

Outwardly they may present well, seem confident and speak eloquently as the need arises, but when it comes to the crunch, they can be found wanting. They lack the commitment, fortitude and sensitivity necessary to accomplish the task. We are all familiar with such people; we've seen them operate and we understand their limitations – all show and no substance.

My advice is to steer clear of them: they deliver no intrinsic value to your organisation and will often have the opposite effect. I once encountered a fellow who used his position as representative purely for personal gain. He had attached himself to an organisation by telling extraordinary tales of having secured major and high-profile sponsors for several other events and properties. When first I met this chap, I knew that all was not as it seemed. He promised the world but they were promises I knew his organisation could not possibly deliver. He was willing to pledge certain benefits that I was aware had been committed elsewhere. His method was to get close to the sponsors, usually through introductions from people known to the sponsorship managers, and then attempt to procure goods and services for his personal use.

Alarm bells rang in the one and only meeting we had when he proceeded to ask me to provide product for his own use. During the discussions he did not once allude to the needs of his organization and at one point even made disparaging remarks about their operational standards. Fortunately I knew several loyal and hardworking members of the organisation in question, and after politely informing them that their representative was not welcome in my office, I advised them that if they sincerely sought sponsorship from my company or any other, they must discard this leech immediately.

I have seen decent and generous sponsors shy away from sponsorship forever after experiencing such types.

Persistence is Bjorn to succeed

'My greatest point is my persistence. I never give up in a match until the last ball. My list of matches shows that I have turned a great many so-called irretrievable defeats into victories.' So speaks five-time winner of the coveted Wimbledon crown Bjorn Borg – someone well qualified to make the point.

Your representative must be willing to fight hard for your interests. You may have a motivated, intelligent and sincere person who does everything right but stops at the first dead end or negative response. I encountered plenty of people like this – good, loyal people with a very genuine desire to succeed in their task but just not able to be persuasive enough to convince sponsorship managers of the value of their offerings. They are going to be far happier and more effective in another role that uses their stronger talents. Your ideal representative must share Bjorn Borg's philosophy. Dogged determination is an attribute worth more to you than a silver tongue or an impressive resume. Cherish it.

I recall one fellow who bounded into my office unannounced. He was representing a sporting body from the small country town of Castlemaine in Victoria, Australia. I had apparently rejected his club's annual request for six pewter tankards that had a total retail value of about $180. One tends to forget that a small request like this can be a major ask for a small club. This gentleman, obviously perplexed by my decision, made the round trip of about 300 kilometres to find out why the request was denied. A phone call would not do this man – it had to be a face-to-face meeting. Firstly, he produced two tins of the famous Castlemaine Rock confectionary, a famous local candy treat, and said, 'Thought I would bring you some Castlemaine Rock. It seems that your company can't afford to buy it, if you have to reject a small request like ours.'

I was speechless. This guy had everything you would want in a representative: guts, tenacity and a passion for his club that drove his actions. What was my reaction? I pulled up a chair for him and we munched on Castlemaine Rock while my assistant parcelled up the tankards. His love of his club was evident in his enthusiastic description of it, in his voice and in his eyes. When he left, I thought how fortunate the club was to have a person of such persistence fronting their sponsorship strategy. I also thought how fortunate I was that there was so few like him doing the sponsorship rounds. As Baltasar Gracián is reputed to have said, 'Put a grain of boldness into everything you do.'

Don't be screened out

On a recent trip to the United States, I telephoned several sponsorship managers in order to introduce myself and to arrange a meeting. On every occasion my call was diverted to a message bank or 'voice mail'. This communications phenomenon is commonplace throughout the world and is used extensively to screen calls. As expected, the pre-recorded greetings asked me to provide my details and the reason for my call and then promised in the most reassuring tones that they would return my calls. Not one call was returned. Expected? Yes! This rather impersonal form of communication is obviously a very effective way of screening calls.

If there is no interest on the part of the sponsorship manager then there is no reason for them to answer. This can be an extremely frustrating exercise on your behalf if you are a trusting individual who still has faith in mankind. Lesser mortals may give up at being snubbed like that. Here I offer a suggestion that may overcome this barrier.

When prompted by the message bank, leave your name and number and advise the manager that you will call back at a certain time. Don't reveal details at this juncture; the point is that you want to provide them personally. Make sure you ring again at the appointed time. Should you encounter the message bank again, leave a similar message and a new time that you will ring. Be persistent: continue until you receive a call. If you have not seen the movie Shawshank Redemption then grab a DVD and enjoy. Without giving away the plot (if you have not seen it), Andy Dufresne (Tim Robbins' character), writes a letter a week to the state government requesting funding for the prison library. After two years he receives boxes of books and a payment of $200 with a request that he write no more. His response was, from that point in time, he would write two letters a week. Persistence pays!

Your persistence will have triggered one of possibly two reactions. The manager has become so annoyed with your tenacity that they have returned your call simply to stop your continual messages. On the other hand, they are impressed by your persistence and their curiosity has been aroused to the point where they want to know what you are after.

Whatever the reason they have for returning your call, you will have succeeded in speaking to the decision maker. Accept nothing less.

A different approach

Another encounter demands a few words. Several years ago, over the course of a few, weeks I received a number of messages that a Bruce Johnstone had called, asking me to call back. This happened to be a period of intense event management; with all my energies and attention already engaged, and as the name meant nothing to me, I consigned the messages to my growing pile of 'things to do when the dust settles'.

One day, just after the last event, I was back at my desk laboriously working my way through the backlog, alone in the office because it was lunchtime and all sensible people were taking that word literally. I heard a knock and looked up to see a gentleman peering into my office.

'G'day,' he said. 'I don't want anything. I just thought I'd like to meet you because I've heard your name around the traps.' What do you say to someone who approaches you like that? I invited him in and learned that he was involved with the Melbourne- based Westside Saints, then a member of the National Basketball League. We chatted for a while and at no time did he ask for anything. A few days later, he rang to invite me to a game and yes, we did end up agreeing to sponsor the Saints.

Bruce's game plan was effective and worked like poison gas. He had tried the obvious route and had met with silence, so he changed his plan, opting for the unusual tack of not making a single request. An informal meeting, a chat, a little bonding then a strategic withdrawal followed by the invitation. He rightly guessed that I had seen all the front-on hard sells and knew that with a little finesse and a lot of persistence, he could achieve more. Bruce believed passionately in his club and what it had to offer, and knew that it could sell itself if given the chance. So he set himself the task of giving it that chance by bringing me to the club to see for myself – and he succeeded. Bruce was a breath of fresh air in my world of hot air and hype.

Bruce became a treasured and trusted friend of mine, and his passing has robbed the world of a loveable and likeable rascal.

Superman's brother

Then there is Mike Bowen, songwriter, poet, author, playwright, raconteur, financial guru, son of Ireland and easily the most punctual person I have ever known. I believe he was born wearing a wristwatch and I could well imagine him berating the midwife for delivering him later than expected. If Mike Bowen says he will ring you at 9 a.m. on a given day, then by God he will ring you at 9 a.m. on that day. And if you have promised likewise and fail to contact him at the appointed time, Mike will call at 9.05 to inquire about your health or any other problems that you might have encountered in missing the call at the appointed and agreed time. This is just an example of his extraordinary attention to detail, which, when coupled with his legendary persistence, is admired and respected by all in the Sponsorship world.

These traits are so apparent and so reliable that he has managed to gain sponsorships where I would have thought the task was impossible. A more passionate individual you could not hope to meet. In short, he exemplifies all that you are looking for in your quest for the superhero representative. Please ensure that you read about him in the case study at the end of this book and as a shameless plug, read his autobiography, "A Time of Secrets."

In conclusion

I do appear to be painting a picture of someone in a splendid blue cape with an 'S' emblazoned on their chest. No, the selection criteria need not include 'can leap tall buildings in a single bound', but the ideal representative is fairly close to a super-person.

They do exist, these people who can change the course of mighty sponsorship policies and bend sponsorship managers with their bare hands – witness our gentleman from Castlemaine – and you might just have one in your organisation.

Of course you may be well satisfied with your organization's representative and in that case, congratulations. But if you have run a more critical eye over your representative and found this person wanting, it is time to identify a replacement – someone who will bring in that vital financial backing and support.

LESSONS TO TAKE FROM THIS CHAPTER

Your representative must be:
- ❖ someone not intimidated by the barriers and blind alleys they might encounter on their way through the maze
- ❖ someone who listens effectively
- ❖ someone who thrives on a challenge
- ❖ someone with confidence, tenacity and a passion for your organisation and its goals, and the drive to see them achieved
- ❖ someone who is unafraid to present your case by phone, by mail or in person
- ❖ someone who is creative in their response to hurdles
- ❖ someone who is utterly reliable.

SUGGESTED RESEARCH EXERCISES

1. Can you identify people in your organisation who possess the traits you are seeking? Furthermore, can you identify those who should *not* be appointed to seek out sponsors?

2. List all the traits you believe should belong to a successful sponsorship seeker. How many do you yourself
possess? How could you improve your abilities so that you could claim to have almost all of those necessary?

FURTHER READING

http://www.scottyoung.com/blog/2008/07/10/building-your-persistence-levels/

How to Be Persistent Without Being Annoying,
http://everydaylife.globalpost.com/persistent-being-annoying-14253.html

http://www.kent.ac.uk/careers/sk/determination.htm

FROM THE EXPERTS

❖ 'By starting the research for sponsors early on and by being persistent you set yourself up not for failure but for success.'

❖ 'A great attitude and persistence are keys to success.'

❖ 'From my point of view, The one word that brings the biggest fear in the hearts of sponsorship seekers in "no." You must remember that the mortality rate for requesting sponsorship is zero. Never fear the "no" word.'

SPONSORSHIP FACT

Following his 2009 Thanksgiving car crash, world champion golfer Tiger Woods suffered a dramatic fall from grace, losing five sponsors and an estimated $50 million in annual income.

WORDS FROM A SPONSORSHIP SEEKER

'I try to establish a routine. I say try, because in this industry it is not always possible. Opportunities pop up at unexpected times. Sponsors require immediate attention. Priorities change in a heartbeat. I have what I call, focus days, where I research potential sponsors. I might develop events and activities that I can match to sponsors' needs and interests, and conduct strategy and brainstorming sessions with my colleagues in order to find new and innovative ways to excite sponsors. My focus days require me to be creative and innovative. This is not always possible but by being aware of sponsors' needs and fully understanding the value that my property has, makes the creative juices flow. Then, I have my out days.

When calling on potential sponsors, I tick off my checklist before I leave the office. Do I have the written proposal, business cards, back up information, pen, lap top and anything else that I need for a professional meeting? Do I have the correct name and title of the prospective sponsor? Am I on time?

When calling on established sponsors, the atmosphere is always less formal, but I never call without having something interesting to show them or to discuss with them. Even if we are meeting informally for lunch or coffee, I will always provide them with information of interest.

Finally, I have my administration days. I usually have lots of large and small different tasks to contend with. Routine tasks such as writing proposals, returning non-urgent phone calls, attending to texts, emails and facebook messages, answering phone call and informal meetings with colleagues and contractors. Most are mundane but all are extremely important to content with.'

Eight

Working with agents

'A visionary is one who can find his way
by moonlight, and see the dawn before
the rest of the world.'
OSCAR WILDE

At this point you may put down the book, asking, Just who do we have in our organisation that can do all of the above? Do we have anyone capable of representing us, of selling the benefits of our events and properties with sufficient professionalism and zeal?

If you cannot find your organisation's ideal representative then you might consider the alternative to an internal appointment – a professional agent. However, before making a decision to contract an agent, you must understand the nature of agents and the services that they can provide. Even if you do not have the money or inclination to invest in one, it is a worthwhile exercise to explore this avenue, if only to exclude it.

The nature of the beast

A sponsorship agent is someone who specialises in consulting, brokering and/or managing sponsorship and/or event relationships. The agent acts as a catalyst in bringing together two parties who have a desire to work together for mutual gain. This is my own brief definition of an agent's core function. There are many permutations of this role, and many other services that agents have to offer.

The function of the beast

A skilled agent will have the ability, knowledge and expertise necessary to help you achieve your goals. They know the maze and all its twists and turns. They can steer you clear of the dead ends and navigate you through the trickier sections that, tackled unaided, might have left you lost and empty-handed. They know where the right matches are to be found for your property and can save you months of serial knock-backs by avoiding the mismatches altogether. They have the 'home maze advantage', if you like. This is only to be expected. After all, you are paying an expert in the field and you have the right to expect that they will transport you to your goal.

All the attributes listed in the previous chapter apply when you are looking for an agent to work for you. But whereas you might have had to settle for compromises on certain points when choosing an insider, you need make no such compromises when paying for the services of an agent. You can expect that your agent will be proficient in assessing your particular needs. They will be adept at identifying the best ways to fill the gaps in your sponsorship hierarchy. Where your sponsors will be ranked within that hierarchy will, of course, be contingent on their order of importance based on the size of the contribution they make to your organisation. Such appraisals by agents can usually be carried out with minimum disruption to your day-to-day operations.

The agent as assessor

Earlier, we looked at the process of auditing your marketable assets, firstly for identification and then for evaluation. The seasoned eye of the experienced agent will often discover areas of opportunity you would never have considered. When using an agent, you have the right to expect that they will accurately assess the value of the property.

An agent will have sufficient experience and exposure to the market to have developed a system of expert evaluation. Those who have been in the business for a long time will have an initial 'gut feel' for the value of a sponsorship package within your category. Through this 'sixth sense' they might form an approximation of the value, but they would rarely go into the marketplace without having married their industry and category pricing knowledge to a methodical audit of your assets. The experienced agent will have a feel for placing the most suitable benefits into a complete package that prospective sponsors will recognise as the right fit for them.

The agent as a key to the door

Imagine the number and quality of contacts a professional agent has at their fingertips – connections to those companies and individuals most active in sponsorship. They should be aware of the precise state of play in the marketplace at any given time. They will be constantly on the alert for news that might affect a company's sponsorship position. Any whisper of a change in fortune or management that might impact on sponsorship dealings will be noted and subsequently reflected in an agent prepared proposal.

The agent may also be aware of organisations that have funds earmarked for sponsorship and are actually on the lookout for the most suitable property. Such companies might be predisposed to evaluating proposals presented by a third and independent party, and may seek submissions from people with whom they have had prior successful dealings and in whom they place their trust. They often hold the well-founded belief that proposals emanating from the office of a particular agent contain fee structures that genuinely reflect the benefits being offered. This is important to the target and to you. If the target knows from experience that this agent will not present a property with an inflated price then they will relax. Their attention will no longer be fixed on the asking price and instead be placed firmly on the tangible benefits offered. In this way, the agent's reputation has removed any doubt about the fairness of the asking fee, and the agent is free to begin the business of building a relationship between you and your new sponsor.

The agent as emissary

As the agent scans the environment for potential sponsors for you and their other clients, you may be assured that they are 'talking you up' to their company contacts. In this way the agent is subtly introducing your organisation and has begun to give a first-hand testimonial on your credibility and commitment to sponsors. They are paving the way for you with organisations that have not heard of you or fully appreciated what you have to offer. If these contacts trust the agent's judgement, your image will rise sharply and they will be open – even eager – to hear more about how you might fit in with their strategies and goals.

The agent in renegotiation

Often an existing sponsor will expect to pay the same fee each year ad infinitum while your organisation sees the matter a little differently. Situations can change. Since the original agreement you might have:

❖ added value to individual deals by granting extra benefits
❖ effected an increase in sales for your exclusive category sponsors by boosting the numbers attending your events
❖ gained greater media coverage for your sponsors and their products through the success of your events or property.

Add to this the effects of inflation, and the fee you negotiated five years ago is worth considerably less today. This is where an agent can be valuable.

They will assist you to revalue your property annually, taking all these points into account. It is part of the agent's brief to gather evidence supporting re-evaluation and to approach sponsors with undeniable evidence that they are receiving benefits in excess of the current fee.

From this stronger ground they will then renegotiate, arriving at a figure based on the added value being enjoyed by your sponsor. Third-party involvement allows you to take a step back from the business end of the arrangement and let your agent wrestle with the sponsor, thereby removing you from the process of haggling over the issues of fees and increases. You remain the 'good guy' and the relationship with your sponsor remains untainted. (For more on renegotiation, see Chapter Sixteen.)

Then there are the problems that can arise when a sponsorship manager leaves a company. The sponsorship arrangement often follows them out of the door. An agent can intervene to prevent this scenario. Clever agents will have well-developed networks within a firm. They will have worked out the accession structure and cultivated the candidates so that they can move quickly when a new manager is appointed. The new manager will be looking for support and, with a relationship of trust already established, might lean on an agent for:

❖ learning about the sponsorship properties
❖ determining the nature of the relationships
❖ seeking introductions to sponsored organisations.

Often the bond between sponsor, event and agent strengthens due to the reliance of the sponsoring body on the agent's expertise.

Identifying the right agent for your organization

The engagement of an agent should not be taken lightly. Your organisation and its needs are important and should not be entrusted to an agent who cannot meet your expectations. You are seeking a champion. Your process of identifying the right person might be protracted as you interview several possibilities before settling on the perfect match. This process may be shortened with – you guessed it – a little research. This time, don't start with the telephone book; ask around. Get testimonials from other organisations that have used agents. Talk to as many people as possible and gradually a list will form. The cream will soon rise to the top of the list because their names recur in these conversations, always in glowing terms. Some will sink to the bottom courtesy of a growing picture of their incompetence or unreliability – these are the ones who will give you heartache and problems you don't need; reject them out of hand. Arrange to meet with those who are repeatedly praised.

When you meet, you will be, in effect, in a two-sided interview. Don't imagine that this person will be 'champing at the bit', begging for your business. The agent will be assessing you and your organisation to determine whether you have potential and whether your properties will have appeal and value for sponsors. If you don't have anything worthwhile to offer a sponsor, the agent will probably walk away, having decided your organization is not going to yield value for effort. An honest agent will acknowledge to you that they do not have the qualifications, time or experience to take on your brief.

The agent will make such judgements at your first meeting, so you will need to have the following information available:
- ❖ the needs of your organization
- ❖ the structure of your organization
- ❖ your reasons for engaging an agent
- ❖ your current sponsorship strategy
- ❖ your current sponsorship strategy
- ❖ the sponsorship funding you require
- ❖ how you intend to use sponsorship funds
- ❖ where you think your event ranks in the minds of sponsors within your event or property category, that is, relative to similar organisations.

While the agent is assessing you and making a judgement call as to whether they want to work for your organisation, you will be equally busy assessing whether they are right for you.

Now it is your opportunity to ask questions and to identify those telltale non-verbal signals that reveal much about the person. Some questions that must be asked at this stage are:
- ❖ Why should I appoint you over the other candidates?
- ❖ Tell me how you go about targeting sponsors for your clients.
- ❖ What can you do for me that I can't do myself?
- ❖ Can you give me the names of three referees for whom you have successfully found sponsors?

After the interview, ask yourself did the agent:
- ❖ Satisfactorily demonstrate expert knowledge in analysing the sponsorship requirements of your organisation?
- ❖ ask about your present and past performance?
- ❖ demonstrate problem-solving techniques?

- ❖ provide examples of success with other clients?
- ❖ speak openly of their dealings with other clients or demonstrate that they can be trusted with confidential information, keeping each client's business private?
- ❖ give hesitant and incomplete answers, or considered, precise and clear answers?
- ❖ fidget, or sit in a calm and poised manner?
- ❖ show a genuine interest in your situation, or was their talk mostly centred on themselves?
- ❖ propose solutions that had been used successfully with other clients or solutions that seemed unique?
- ❖ offer testimonials of their services?
- ❖ give you the impression that they are proficient in their work and effective as a person?

Determining the agent's fees

If you feel that the agent meets your requirements and believe that they can benefit your organisation, it is time to engage them. This may prove costly, but presumably you have weighed the benefits against the costs and found that the investment will be worthwhile. How much and how you pay for the service is closely related to the quality of person you retain. Don't imagine that the lowest priced agent can offer you the same value as a highly priced one: they may not have the same motivation, experience or energy. Negotiate a fair price and always remember that if you pay peanuts you are most likely to get monkeys.

Commission basis

In most cases your agent should be retained on a commission basis that is, paid on the fee structure of any new sponsorship deal they negotiate. The normal rate is between 15 and 20 per cent of the sponsorship fee.

When this is relatively low, it may be appropriate to raise the agent's fee as their time and effort is similar regardless of the size of the deal. Conversely, and using the same logic, the percentage may be set at a lower rate when the negotiated sponsorship fee is high. Figure 9 is meant as a guide only. Fees are always linked to the event or property and will vary accordingly.

Table 9: Guide to agents' fees.

NEGOTIATED EVENT FEE	AGENT'S PERCENTAGE	AGENT'S FEE
$5000	20	$1000
$10000	17.5	$1750
$50000	15	$6000

Retainer basis

Some organisations rely heavily on their agent, using them not simply to secure sponsorship, but to administer their entire sponsorship portfolio. They authorise the agent to audit the organization's assets, formulate budgets, liaise with sponsors, handle the day-to-day administration, renegotiate expiring agreements, write proposals and plan future sponsorship strategies. In essence, they have outsourced management of all their sponsorship issues. In effect the agent is the designer and custodian of your sponsorship relationships and as such you should expect to pay them a reasonable retainer.

Disadvantages of using agents

Although there may be many advantages in engaging an agent, I also believe that there is often a strong case against it. Many companies like the personal touch and enjoy dealing directly with an organisation. They may cite the following reasons for not wanting an agent involved in negotiations:

- ❖ They don't trust agents (perhaps due to an unpleasant past experience).
- ❖ They believe that commission fees paid to agents are dead monies from which neither sponsor nor sponsored benefit.
- ❖ They feel that commission fees raise the cost of entering into a sponsorship relationship without adding any value.

I must admit that I always preferred to deal directly with the sponsored organisation, mainly because I am a 'people-person'. I also feel I gained far greater insight into a property or event when I was dealing with those 'on the ground'. Yet there is nothing as exhilarating as negotiating vigorously with a thoroughly professional and dedicated agent, and finding the win–win conclusion.

A word of caution

In the foregoing discussion I have been speaking of the 'ideal' agent – one whose talent and professional reputation precede them. But, of course, like any other profession there is such a thing as a dishonest agent. A trained eye can spot one of the disreputable types fairly easily, as they have an unmistakable aura about them. These are self-interest agents. Many approached me; few got what they expected.

Two such characters are indelibly printed on my memory. One became incensed when I told him the benefits he was offering were not sufficient for the fee. He ranted and stamped about the office and it became transparently clear that he had no interest in the property – all this anger was about his commission.

A second agent was offering me a certain minor event when he realised I had funds available for major sponsorships. He immediately told me to forget the property he had been representing and began selling another, higher-priced property as fast and as hard as he could. I felt sorry for the people who thought he was there with their interests at heart. They would have been horrified to see how quickly he dropped them when he sensed the probability of a larger commission.

If you are unused to this field, these operators may appear to be genuine. They probably have a slick line of patter and ooze charm. Let them by their deeds be judged. Always check with people who have used them before. There must be a proven and impressive track record before you give your money and your sponsorship prospects to any agent.

LESSONS TO TAKE FROM THIS CHAPTER

- ❖ Professional sponsorship agents play in the maze all day so they know it inside out.
- ❖ An agent can be a buffer between you and the sponsor when it is time to renegotiate.
- ❖ Appointing an agent is a big step – take the time to make the right selection.
- ❖ Be aware that in sponsorship, as in all fields, there are those out for a 'fast buck'.

SUGGESTED RESEARCH EXERCISES

- ❖ Make inquiries among colleagues and friends about their use of, and experience with, agents of any kind. Ask the respondents to list all the best qualities and undesirable traits they found in these agents. Listen to all the horror stories as well as the glowing testimonials. Review this information and see what you now think of agents. If you decide to proceed with the appointment of an agent you will now have greater understanding of what you are looking for – and not looking for.

❖ Try to find out if your target sponsor likes to deal direct or through an agent.

SPONSORSHIP FACT

Revenue generated by commercial partnerships accounts for more than 40 percent of Olympic revenues and partners provide vital technical services and product support to the whole of the Olympic Family. Each level of sponsorship entitles companies to different marketing rights in various regions, category exclusivity and the use of designated Olympic images and marks.

Nine

Finding and accessing the right person

'You can't hit a home run unless you step up to the plate. You can't catch a fish unless you put your line in the water. You can't reach your goals if you don't try.'
KATHY SELIGMAN

Now you understand a little about the ebb and flow – and odd tsunami – in the world of sponsorship, it is time you understood the person at the sponsorship helm of any large organisation. That person is the one you will deal with and is therefore the one you must know and understand.

Inside contacts

Like any good maze, the sponsorship one has blind alleys and false trails. From my experience there are many people within companies who can read and evaluate proposals and conduct discussions with prospective sponsorship partners. For example, a customer might approach a sales representative of the company and ask if they could organise a sponsorship for the local football club. A finance manager might be asked by his daughter's netball team to provide sponsorship through his company. Or the company's production supervisor might be approached for support by a friend who works for a charity organisation. All these contacts may seem important, and they are a link into a potential sponsor's domain, but they are good starting points only and certainly not the end of your efforts.

The truth is that most of these promising connections do not have the authority to approve your proposal. More often than not, they will refer your request to a higher authority, and usually without the same passion that you would have used if pitching the proposal yourself. In 99 per cent of cases, all this will generate is a standard 'no' letter. Then, if you go back to your contact, they will say, 'Gosh my friend, I gave it my best shot . . . We just missed out because the company had already allocated this year's funds . . . Give it to me again next year – a little earlier.' The truth is that they probably did give it ***their*** best shot; they were just not in the position to give it ***the*** best shot. The problem is that you don't want to strain the relationship or embarrass your contact by now approaching someone else in the organisation. From your point of view, you have lost your chance with this company. Failure! Back to square one!

My company sales representatives would often tell me that customers had approached them with proposals. 'Don't worry. I've handled it,' they would assure me. 'I told them you would probably have said no.' What a disaster for the sponsorship seeker! They are left with the impression that someone in a position to do so has appraised their proposal and turned it down. But for the sake of a little research and a personal approach to the decision maker, the result might have been very different.

There is usually one person with whom you must negotiate and that person is the one with the power and authority to accept and approve your proposal. Find out who that person is and make your approach to them.

The person with the power of 'yes'

Before approaching any potential sponsor, you need to find answers to these questions:
- ❖ Who is the ultimate decision maker?
- ❖ Is it the sponsorship manager?
- ❖ Do they show any personal preferences towards a certain type of property?
- ❖ Do they prefer proposals to be forwarded only after an initial phone discussion or faxed outline?
- ❖ Will your proposal be read by someone less able to make a decision?
- ❖ Do they have any preferred time for calls? For example, are they always in the office and available on Thursday mornings?
- ❖ Are they about to go on holidays? (If so, your proposal may sit around unread for a considerable time or

Make sure the information is reliable

The way to find the answers is to conduct some basic research. If you have the appropriate contact within a target organisation, of course use them – but as a source of information, rather than as your sole contact. If your relationship is a strong one based on mutual respect and reciprocity, they will usually be only too happy to help. They will know, or can find out, who the decision maker is, and may even have the influence to arrange an introduction to or an interview with this person.

Be warned, however. Information may be readily available, but not always reliable, so verify everything. Information about who holds what position in a company always has a use-by date. Make sure that you have today's intelligence, not yesterday's. And consider how close to the source your informant is. The more people in an information chain, the more distorted the message received by the final link will be.

Consider the old story about the message sent by a military general to headquarters via several runners: 'Send reinforcements, we're going to advance.' Legend has it that when the message arrived at headquarters it had become, 'Send three and four pence, we're going to a dance.'

Don't get caught out by Chinese whispers!

The message here is, Do your homework and do it thoroughly. Research time is never wasted. Use the methods described in Chapter Three to collect and analyse the available data on your target company's sponsorship manager.

The busy life of a sponsorship manager

Once you have found the sponsorship manager, it is essential that you appreciate and are sensitive to this person's pressures. This is the point at which many people fail to grasp the reality of the situation. They imagine the sponsorship manager sitting, hands clasped, at an empty desk, waiting for their call. When their first attempt at contact yields nothing, they feel rejected. With an attitude like that, they are risking enormous distress if things do not proceed according to their script. The faint-hearted will bail out at this point and try the same 'crash through or crash' approach elsewhere (probably with similar results), working their way down a shrinking list of target sponsors. (We shouldn't judge them too harshly, though, because they have obviously not had the benefit of reading this book!) One of the most important things you should take from these pages is an understanding of what a sponsorship manager's job entails. If you know with whom you are dealing and what pressures they are under, you will be better equipped.

The sponsorship manager's working day

In the times I occupied the sponsorship chairs at both CUB and at the

Mayne Group, I was for many people as elusive as an absconded expatriate entrepreneur.

When someone finally managed to get through to me, there would be the inevitable, 'Oh, you really do exist!' or 'I've increased the profits for my telephone provider. It's taken me many, many calls to reach you.'

Unfortunately, I knew their complaints had a basis. I must say in my defense, and in the defense of all others who hold a sponsorship position, that my work schedule was so full that I wonder how *anyone* got through.

The average sponsorship manager moves through the day with all the sedate and dignified calm of the Tazzie Devil cartoon character of 'Bugs Bunny Show' fame. The initial barrage of phone calls and messages continues unabated throughout the day. The mail brings as many as forty new proposals, and more arrive via the fax, courier service and e-mail. All require evaluation and a reply – either a standard 'thanks but no thanks' or an invitation to meet for further discussions.

Internal and external correspondence both require action and response, and then the daily round of meetings begins: meetings with prospective and existing sponsorship recipients; meetings with sign writers and function caterers; meetings to arrange trophies, photography, uniforms . . . And then there are the actual events to attend and 'fly the corporate flag'. Meanwhile, back at the office life goes on, with more proposals, more correspondence.

Should an interstate or overseas visit take the manager away from the office for a couple of days or even weeks, the backlog waiting when they are next at their desk seems almost insurmountable.

And you're telling me that you want to pin this person down and pitch your fabulous proposal without delay? Don't despair. It's all a matter of timing. When is the best time to make an appointment? When will your decision maker be in peak reception mode? Being receptive to ideas and approaches is a state of mind and we are all subject to peaks and troughs in receptivity.

Factors that have an impact on an individual's receptivity may be unpredictable – we can have no idea of what sort of day this person is going to have, or what might intrude on it five minutes before your appointment that might dramatically increase or decrease receptivity. But on a broader, more general level there will be times of the day or week when the ebbs and flows are more predictable – and you can manipulate this knowledge.

To give you some idea, consider my experience regarding scheduling presentations and interviews. Mondays were usually best left well alone. If I had attended functions and events during the weekend, I preferred to take Monday to regroup. It was usually a day to clean up any backlog and attempt to balance the coming week's schedule. Likewise, I avoided Fridays, which I needed to finalise arrangements for the approaching weekend's sponsored events and usually had a lunchtime meeting or preparation session.

So on Tuesdays to Thursdays I was a little less distracted and therefore more open to appointments and presentations. Even on these days the optimum time was 8.30 a.m. until just before lunch-time. Afternoons were usually reserved for internal meetings, event management and proposal evaluations.

When you are speaking to the sponsorship manager or their assistant, listen carefully to the days and times they suggest. Where possible, slot yourself in as the first or last appointment of a session. Like it or not, these are the ones that are easiest for the manager to recall. The people in the middle tend to be a blur of faces, presentations and proposals, while the last presentation tends to be the one that the manager takes away with them. I often used to discuss the last presentation with my colleagues at lunch because it was uppermost in my mind.

The sponsorship manager in crisis

During a period of siege such as the 'beer wars' outlined in Chapter Two, the sponsorship manager is totally absorbed in the current crisis. They will channel every bit of time into that situation, striving to ensure that the company and brand do not weaken or forfeit ground in the shake-out. Asking for an audience with someone immersed in conflict would be akin to asking for a miracle.

I don't tell you this to impress you with a sense of the sponsorship manager's importance, but to help you better Understand when an approach is appropriate. You must develop the flexibility and finesse to identify such situations and evaluate the present state of your target. This is not the time to make an approach – wait until the dust settles. If you have already commenced negotiations and such a situation arises, tell your target you are happy to suspend discussions until things are calmer. Be assured that they will be grateful for the breathing space and will certainly not forget your gesture when negotiations recommence.

Remember, they need your approach

Be assured that the sponsorship manager is not deliberately avoiding you or disinclined to listen to your pitch. In most cases the reverse is true. They will want to, and quite possibly need to, consider your proposal, because seeking out strategically advantageous properties is an important part of their job description. Until they have read your proposal or interviewed you, they do not know what you can offer them. It may be that you have the very proposal they need – the one that will enhance consumer attitudes to their product and increase their market share.

Sponsorship managers build their reputations on their ability to find the right partners for their organisations to sponsor. Their continued standing and value to their employers depends on that skill. They must continually scan the horizon, keep up with industry trends and predict future threats. Therefore, it is in their own best interests to at least scan all proposals that cross their desk – including yours.

Be persistent

Just as there are ways to move beyond all the difficulties you encounter in the maze, there are methods and mechanisms that will help and encourage you to secure meaningful discussions with the sponsorship manager. The message is: be persistent. I know this might appear to sound like a simplistic solution for a difficult problem, but never underestimate its worth.

Michael Jordan, arguably one of the most gifted athletes of the twentieth century, said: 'Obstacles don't have to stop you. If you run into a brick wall, don't turn around and give up. Figure out how to climb it, go through it or work around it.'

Persistence is an admirable trait and an attribute transferable to most situations in life. To the majority of decision makers, persistence is a sign that you have faith and confidence in your organisation and are convinced of the mutual value in the proposed partnership. Far from being branded a nuisance, people with that magic attribute will often be given a hearing simply because their tenacity is admired. Persistence is born of passion and vision and can be seen in the eyes, heard in the voice and felt in the presence of someone truly committed to an organisation.

If you give up after the first few unsuccessful phone calls, you risk failing to secure a sponsorship or ending up in an alliance with a company that is either not philosophically aligned with your organisation or not sufficiently resourced to meet your needs. Neither party takes optimum benefit from a friction between ideologies or a mismatch of need.

In conclusion

All the people I have met who hold sponsorship positions are approachable 'people people'. Those who fill these positions are usually outgoing and open. The sponsorship manager is neither a masked man or woman, nor a mysterious mirage. They are simply a person doing a job, working long hours usually under enormous pressure and always burdened with severe time constraints.

By setting up a program of initial research and sponsorship targeting, you will identify the right company, the right time, the right approach and the right person – the one with the power of yes. You will have eliminated many of the possible corridors to a rejection and at least have found the right pathway in. By identifying the paths you need to tread, you are starting to put together an idea of the best route to take. You have broken your task down into a sequence of steps that make the whole less daunting. Already you have rounded a corner or two of the maze.

Now let's press ahead.

LESSONS TO TAKE FROM THIS CHAPTER

- ❖ Research, research, research.
- ❖ Qualify and verify all second-, third- and fourth-hand information and ensure it is up to date.
- ❖ Identify the decision maker and discover how they work.
- ❖ Sponsorship managers are busy people. Make allowances for this when trying to make contact with them, and ensure you make that contact during their periods of optimal receptivity.
- ❖ Sponsorship managers are always on the lookout for new opportunities to increase their product's profile.
- ❖ Be persistent – it is the key to success.
- ❖ Don't panic and never give up. Remember – there are no losers, just winners who quit too soon.

SUGGESTED RESEARCH EXERCISE

Consider the activities you fit into an average day.

- ❖ How do you allocate your time in terms of travel, work, entertainment / leisure and rest?
- ❖ You will most likely decide that the work component accounts for quite a sizeable proportion of your day and that it keeps you quite busy. Now ask yourself how you would cope with the pressure if you added an additional load to your work timetable. How would you handle another twenty phone calls (average duration of three minutes per call) and four additional appointments (fifteen minutes duration) added to your schedule?
- ❖ Draw up a schedule showing how you currently allocate your work time in an average day. Now draw up a second schedule and include the extra calls and appointments, but be sure to program them into the existing time allocation. As you attempt this exercise you will find it requires adept and disciplined time management skills. It will also give you an indication of the time constraints most sponsorship managers are up against!

VIGNETTE

Probably the greatest example of persistence is Abraham Lincoln. If you want to learn about somebody who did not quit, look no further.

Born into poverty, Lincoln was faced with defeat throughout his life. He lost 8 elections, twice failed in business and suffered a nervous breakdown. He could have quit many times - but he didn't.

Because he didn't quit, he became one of the greatest Presidents in the history of US. Lincoln was a champion and he never gave up. Here is a sketch of Lincoln's road to the White House:
- ❖ 1816 : His family was forced out of their home. He had to work to support them.
- ❖ 1818 : His mother died.
- ❖ 1831 : Failed in business.
- ❖ 1832 : Ran for state legislature - Lost.
- ❖ 1832 : Lost his job. Wanted to go to law school, but couldn't get in.
- ❖ 1833 : Borrowed some money from a friend to begin business, but became bankrupt by the year end.
- ❖ 1834 : Ran for state legislature again - Won.
- ❖ 1835 : Was engaged to be married, but his fiancée died.
- ❖ 1836 : Had a total nervous breakdown and was in bed for 6 months.
- ❖ 1838 : Sought to become speaker of the state legislature - Defeated.
- ❖ 1840 : Sought to be elector - Defeated.

- ❖ 1843 : Ran for Congress - Lost.
- ❖ 1846 : Ran for Congress again. This time he won. Went to Washington and did a good job.
- ❖ 1848 : Ran for re-election to Congress - Lost.
- ❖ 1849 : Sought the job of land officer in his home state - Rejected.
- ❖ 1854 : Ran for the Senate of the US - Lost.
- ❖ 1856 : Sought the Vice-Presidential nomination at his party's national convention - Got less than 100 votes.
- ❖ 1858 : Ran for the US Senate again - Lost again.
- ❖ 1860 : Elected President of the US.

Lincoln's persistence echoed, "Quitters Never Win and Winners Never Quit."

FURTHER READING

Why Quitting Should Never Be An Option,
http://www.success.bz/articles/7781/why_quitting_should_never_be_an_opt
ion

Building your persistence levels,
http://www.scotthyoung.com/blog/2008/07/10/building-your-persistence-levels/

Don't Underestimate the Value of Good Information,
http://connstep.wordpress.com/2010/03/03/don%E2%80%99t-underestimate-the-value-of-good-information/

ANOTHER WORD ON PATIENCE

Remember that patience is a virtue. Being patient is a trait that can be difficult to master. It is never easy and can be frustrating. This is a world where everything is instant this and immediate that: it is not fashionable to be patient. However patience is a virtue that can be cultivated and nurtured.

Starting his writing career at the age of 27 years, it took Mark Twain 23 years until he produced time honoured *The Adventures of Huckleberry Finn*. He understood the virtue of patience! After a slow start because he had never painted frescoes previously, Michelangelo took over four years (July 1508 - October 1512) to paint the Sistine Chapel. He understood the virtue of patience! My own Golden Retriever, Mindy, knows that barking or whining or running around will not get her feed any quicker. She understands (in a doggy sense) the virtue of patience!

Sponsorship fact

The first recorded example of a sports sponsorship was that of the 1861 first England cricket tour to Australia. The British catering company, Spiers and Pond sponsored the tour.

Ten

The offer they can't refuse – the proposal

'Spectacular achievement is always preceded by
spectacular preparation.'
ROBERT H. SCHULLER

Ernest Hemingway, famous writer and fisherman, put it well: 'The first draft of anything is shit,' he once said. Using Mr. Hemingway's colourful description as a guide, I would have to say that over the years many 'first drafts' crossed my desk.

Many organisations fail to comprehend the importance of the document that is essentially the first contact between prospective sponsors and themselves. Consequently, little care or imagination is invested in its preparation. When sponsorship managers peruse a proposal that is obviously a first draft, their thought processes turn it into images of unprofessional and difficult-to-deal-with organisations.

Once the alarm bells begin to ring, your chances of success dwindle. Give yourself a reasonable chance; ensure that your proposal is professional, polished and contains no fatal flaws. In other words, it must pass the scrutiny of very professional and skilled sponsorship managers. During the first read, any discrepancies, anomalies or defects will propel your document to the rejection pile.

Never send a first draft to anyone yet alone a proposed sponsor!

Adopt the same principles as the sponsorship manager and make sure that your proposal is a professional document reflecting the professionalism of your organisation. Rewrite and refine as many times as necessary to produce the 'perfect' document. To cite an example, this book bears absolutely no resemblance to my first draft. Why? Because it was rewritten and edited over and over until it was felt that we had produced a polished and professional book worthy of being published. Your task is to do exactly the same. The risks are high but the rewards are well worth the extra effort.

> "If I had eight hours to chop down a tree, I would spend six hours sharpening my axe."
> Abraham Lincoln.

Very wise words Mr. President. A well prepared axe will make the task of chopping down a tree much easier and probably safer. Using Abe's words in a sponsorship quest context, you would do well in spending more time in preparing your proposal than in actually writing it.

Format, design and delivery

Like the humans that put them together, proposals come in all shapes and sizes. They can be made:

- ❖ Verbally
- ❖ in a short or a longer letter
- ❖ as a bound full-colour presentation with photographs
- ❖ as mock-ups of posters and other promotional material with the potential sponsor's logo prominently in place
- ❖ as combinations of the above
- ❖ as a video or computer-generated presentation using software such as PowerPoint or Freelance Graphics.

They can arrive on a sponsorship manager's desk in just as many ways: by post (now rather unfairly dubbed 'snail mail' by electronic wizards) by e-mail or facsimile transmission hand-delivered by a professional courier service or a representative of the applicant organisation.

Dressing it up

Many organisations agonise over the format and design of their proposal. Some pay a king's ransom to have it professionally produced, believing that the sponsorship manager will be so mesmerised by the beauty of their document that they will draw up a contract without even opening it.

No matter what the format, size, colour or mode of arrival, it was always the content and substance that I was interested in. These are the key elements in what is basically a 'selling' document.

Your proposal must paint a vivid picture of the viability of your organisation and its proposed relationship with the potential sponsor. This will open up to you the centre of the maze, where you finally have the chance to plead your case personally. The proposal is of vital importance, so don't skimp on effort when drawing it up. Prepare it as you would prepare yourself for a job interview or a special date – dress to impress, but don't leave it to the clothes alone to secure the job or the goodnight kiss.

Consider a job interview situation. Many applicants are smart enough to get the job. Many have the same qualifications as you, or even better. How will you be remembered when the last person leaves the interview room – great suit, shame about the skills deficit?

What are the essentials?

A secret from one who knows: when they strip away the gloss and razzamatazz, or read between the lines, there are three major things sponsorship managers want to find out. It will be these three elements that gain an invitation to proceed further or generate a polite letter of refusal:
- ❖ What is the property on offer?
- ❖ What support does the organisation want?
- ❖ What benefit does my company get for its support?

Of course there are many other factors that the sponsorship manager will consider before reaching a final decision, but if your proposal does not contain the answers to these questions it may be rejected already.

What the experts look for in the content of a proposal

When I asked my survey respondents about proposal content, the general message was that they wanted to receive as much pertinent information as possible, presented in a concise and easily digested form. Some wanted the document to concentrate on providing evidence of the value and worth of the sponsorship deal to their organisation. Others looked for a clear and well-defined argument stating why their company should sponsor this property.

They were looking for an indication that the proposer had done the necessary homework and could demonstrate why the alliance was the right 'fit' for both parties.

A few sponsors said that their main concern was the bottom line: What is the fee? These managers were almost certainly working from the 'affordable' method of sponsorship budgeting, that is, allocating a sum to sponsorships and evaluating only those proposals that fell within those budget parameters. There was a general consensus that most organisations are becoming more professional in their approach for sponsorship funding but that there is still a long way to go. It seems that even the highest-quality proposals lack the clarity and detail that managers would like to see. Many organisations fail in their quest at the first reading because they do not give enough information for the sponsorship manager to make a quick decision that will elevate them to the next stage of review. Respondents said that given time constraints, they did not have the luxury of being able to chase information unless sponsoring the property offered something critical to their business objectives.

Presenting your case

When I was a young man, I worked for the public service. One day I overheard an intriguing exchange. My boss was trying to explain to Henry, a fellow clerk, how he wanted certain documents filed. Try as he might, he could not get Henry to understand. With all due respect to Henry, he was certainly not the sharpest knife in the drawer. Finally, in exasperation, my boss arranged the files in three stacks and asked Henry what he had for dinner each night. 'Soup, main course and dessert,' came the rather bemused reply.

The boss continued on this puzzling theme. 'What order do you have them in?' 'I start with the soup . . . then I have the main course, and then I have dessert.' The boss pointed to the first pile. 'This is the soup. This is the main course,' he said, pointing to the second pile. 'And here', he jabbed a finger at the last stack, 'is the dessert. Now go and file these documents – and start with the soup.' My boss wanted the filing done in a logical sequence, for ease of retrieval and insurance against any document going astray.

Sponsorship managers are no different. No matter how fancy, intricate or ingenious your proposal seems to be, make sure that it is lucid and flows in a logical sequence so that it leads the reader effortlessly through from opening sentence to concluding statement. The last thing you would want is for the reader to throw down the document and say, 'What on earth was that all about?'

When asked what I want in a proposal, my answer is simple:
- ❖ What have you got? (the soup)
- ❖ What do you want? (the main course)
- ❖ What's in it for me? (the dessert)

Giving yourself the edge

Hooking a sponsor is a competitive business. So many baiting their hooks; so few fish! At any time proposals are piled high in the in-trays and out-trays of sponsorship managers everywhere. Often there is not a great deal separating the least attractive and the most worthy. So why yours? What will it be that differentiates yours from its rivals? In other words, where is your competitive edge? I advise putting all you've got into the first section: lead with your offer – the 'what have you got?' or 'soup' part of the proposal.

The soup

Make this strong and attractive. Here you should explain who you are, so it is best to:
- ❖ lead with a brief but attractive description of your organisation, its aims and charter, to provide the reader with a basic background so they understand who you are and what you are about
- ❖ summarise the sorts of things your organisation is involved in
- ❖ outline the event or property that is available for sponsorship and why it is so valuable that if it is not snatched up by the reader, someone else will surely rip it out from under their procrastinating nose.

The way you present this information should be compelling, and it should stimulate the reader's attention.

Ideally, it will arouse three very important feelings: awareness, interest and curiosity. The very first page of the document should proceed something like this: Start with a catchy opening such as those in Figure 10, which will entice your reader to read on. Place the target sponsor within the proposal – make them integral to it. Use inclusive language, second-person pronouns, 'you', 'your', 'we' and 'our'. Use terms such as 'your opportunity' rather than 'this opportunity' and 'your sponsorship benefits' instead of 'the sponsorship benefits'.

This technique personally involves the reader. A small thing, but a good move psychologically. In this way you will hope to develop in the reader a sense of ownership before the fact. Keep it simple but arouse the reader's AIC (awareness, interest and curiosity) with the soup, and they will look for a generous helping of MIP (more information please) in the main course.

In short, you will have whetted their appetite.

Figure 10: Attention-grabbing headlines.

**ACTORS PLAYHOUSE OFFERS
FRUIT GUM COMPANY
THE SWEETEST OPPORTUNITY OF A LIFETIME**
♠
THERE ARE THOUSANDS OF
NEW CUSTOMERS WAITING FOR YOU AT THE FINISH POST
AT KANSAS CITY HORSERACING CLUB
♠
**TARGET YOUR CUSTOMERS
BY SUPPORTING
THE RED CROSS**
♠
BMW AND THE BARKLY MANCHESTER WANDERERS
A BETTER MATCH THAN
CORN FLAKES AND MILK
♠
**SUPPORT SURF LIFESAVING –
AND LEAVE COMPETITORS IN YOUR WAKE**
♠
YOU ARE CORDIALLY INVITED TO MAKE A HOMELESS PERSON
FEEL LIKE THEY HAVE A HOME THIS CHRISTMAS –
SUPPORT THE MAYOR'S ANNUAL APPEAL

The main course

The main course is where you tell them what you want. In this section you should nominate what support you are looking for: cash, products, services . . . I would strongly recommend that you justify the amount you are asking for, showing how much will be spent where. For example, you might be looking to stage a charity ball. Once you have justified the need for the ball and the benefits your organisation will get from it, set out the cost breakdown, showing which areas – for example, catering or venue – with which you seek assistance.

Proposals do arrive without such detail, but when it is included it shows that you have done your sums and know your business – that you haven't simply plucked a figure out of the air. A suspicion that the figure has been arrived at through guesswork can be unsettling to the sponsorship manager: if you have overestimated, you are taking money you will not need; if you have underestimated, you may not be able to deliver all you promise.

Careful costing has another immediate benefit. Sponsorship managers love to bargain and might not accept your asking fee at once. The formula I used when evaluating a proposal was to read it through and weigh up the strategic benefits against the asking price. I would then reduce the asking fee to 25 per cent of its total and read the proposal again, weighing up the strategic benefits against this reduced amount. If I believed that the property could be delivered at the lesser price, then I would make an offer at the discounted rate. This method was successful (for me) in the majority of cases, although there were times when I was forced to increase the offer. On the whole, though, I found it was unusual to have to pay the full price asked.

On those rare occasions when proposals spelt out exactly how the fee would be allocated and included an extensive budget and costing sheet to justify the request, I had less room to manoeuvre. Yes, there was still the obligatory haggling process with all the passion and fire you might see at an Arab street bazaar, but in the end the property would usually receive an amount not dissimilar to the one originally requested.

The dessert

The difference between this sort of meal and the real thing is that the richer the fare consumed in the first and second courses, the more the sponsorship manager is looking forward to dessert – what's in it for us?

This is the section where your homework pays off. It is where the information you have prepared about the target is applied. List all the benefits and advantages – direct and indirect – the target can expect to receive by accepting your proposal. These may include sales gains, competitive advantages, networking opportunities and entry into new markets. Whatever areas of sponsors' interest you have discovered during your research, now is the time to introduce them. Show your target that they will get top value per dollar spent on you.

How much proposal is enough?

Not long after the city of Adelaide announced it had snared a round of the Formula One Grand Prix, I received a proposal from a well-known F1 racing-car manufacturer. It was a one-page letter of three brief paragraphs.

The first paragraph stated that the company could construct a racing car for my company; the second revealed the sum such a car would cost us and the third promised that the car would be ready for the first Adelaide Grand Prix.

Although it did not follow the flow suggested above, it described our proposed relationship in clear and concise terms. But I had a problem with the price – $10 million – given the amount of detail provided, which was almost nil. Surely someone receiving a request for such a vast sum could reasonably expect that it would be accompanied by a detailed breakdown of the proposal.

I have also been handed proposals for relatively small amounts which read like an illustrated *War and Peace:* reams of paper with colour photos and mock-ups. So just how much detail is needed if the reader is to be satisfied?

Keep your documentation proportionate to the amount sought. You might find this difficult. You might want to give every shred of information to the sponsorship manager – but a cumbersome, overdone document could well meet with precisely the opposite reaction to the one hoped for. If the reader can't get to the heart of the matter quickly, chances are they will put your proposal aside to be perused later. And your chances immediately take a nosedive. 'Later' could be weeks away; meanwhile, another proposal in a like category but couched in simple, concise terms might arrive, and be read, followed up and approved. Ninety seconds was all the time I allowed a proposal to catch my interest. I received too many to devote any more time to analyzing their value. Work on the KISS principle: Keep it simple, stupid.

Explain your proposal in clear, concise English. Don't get tangled up in long, complicated explanations – I've read proposals of such complexity that I have had to put them aside and take a deep breath. Your aim is to keep the reader's optimal interest and understanding until the last full stop. A sponsorship manager who has to plough through intricate, verbose and convoluted descriptions is not a happy sponsorship manager, and your 90 seconds of attention will have been wasted. Not enough, or too much – it is a fine balancing act. My best advice is that you present the information in such a way that the reader can answer the three questions 90 seconds after they have picked it up:

❖ What's on offer?
❖ What do you want?
❖ What's in it for my company?

Getting it right

The computer and its ability to provide us with the marvels of word processing is a truly wondrous invention – how did Tolstoy manage without it? With this tool we can save time using a host of applications including basic layouts and mail merge, and we are able to correct spelling errors and use the thesaurus (judiciously) to choose just the right word for every occasion. It facilitates correspondence, communication and accuracy to such a degree that any problems that do arise rest squarely in the hands of the operator. Is this testimonial to technology relevant to the subject in hand? Yes, very much so. I have seen some of the most basic mistakes in proposals: errors that should never have been allowed to go unchecked and uncorrected; errors that might have cost proposals any chance of success.

Check the name, title and address of your target

One morning I examined my mail and found an envelope that was correctly addressed to me:

Postage
Paid
50 cents

Mr. Mike Turner,
Sponsorship Manager – Southern States,
Carlton & United Breweries Ltd.,
GPO Box 753F,
Melbourne. 3001.
Australia.

I opened it and read the cover letter. The name, title and address at the top of the page were correct, but the body of the letter started:
'Dear Mr. Tuna . . .'
Thoughts of lunch had apparently taken precedence over the important process of proofreading. Fortunately, I found the slip amusing and showed the faux pas to my colleagues, who, it should be said, milked the mistake for all it was worth. Not all recipients of such a mistake will be amused. For many, a 'Dear Mr. Tuna' letter will be consigned to the rubbish bin, along with its sender's aspirations.

Be specific

Sometimes letters crossed my desk with the vaguest information on the envelope: 'The manager', 'To whom it may concern' or 'The sponsorship department' were three regulars. It always amazed me that someone seeking financial support and a relationship with my company had not bothered to take the few minutes needed to find out the name and title of the person to whom the correspondence should have been addressed.

In a large company a letter that is not specifically addressed will go straight to the mail room or central records office to be opened by clerks whose job it is to determine, from the letter's contents, where it should be forwarded. In some cases, these letters will bounce around the system for weeks, landing in one wrong department after another before touching down at their intended destination. They finally arrive, dog-eared and worn, often after the date for which the funding was requested, or at least too late for the sponsor to arrange the signage, merchandising or advertising needed. Another opportunity goes begging.

Although my correct title was 'Sponsorship Manager – Southern States', I had a variety of titles bestowed on me by poorly informed people during my time in that role:
- ❖ Managing Director
- ❖ Marketing Director
- ❖ Sponsorship Director
- ❖ Sales Director
- ❖ General Manager

Mostly quite flattering, but all incorrect. Apart from the common courtesy angle, a wrongly addressed letter is evidence that the sender does not know who you are or what your title is – and doesn't really care enough to find out. In these cases I wondered whether the shotgun mail-out method had been used and how many copies of exactly the same proposal were received by other companies. In using the generic letter approach, you have failed to customise the proposal to the needs and aims of the target companies and failed to use your research effectively.

The right envelope

Here's another horror story. One day I received a proposal properly addressed with my name and title correct. When I opened the envelope, however, the letter inside was to my counterpart at another company. I can only guess that at the same time he was reading a letter that started 'Dear Mr. Turner' (or, possibly, Tuna). When the letters were swapped (which would not necessarily happen – they may simply be thrown away), they were identical. It is difficult to recover from such a memorable gaffe and almost impossible to achieve a successful outcome when the target has formed an adverse opinion of your professional attitude before they have read past the envelope and greeting.

E-proposals

A word of warning about sending your proposal by e-mail. The easy access and immediacy of this method have much appeal, but e-mail addresses resemble a formula for nuclear fission. Addressed wrongly – missing a vital dot or misplacing an @ – and the all important letter will boomerang, causing the very delay you were hoping to avoid by sending it electronically. Nowadays a lot of emails sent to companies are dispatched to SPAM files, destined new to be opened or read.

In conclusion

This part of the maze should not be particularly tricky; you need no special skill to negotiate it, beyond a commitment to courtesy and some common sense. Double-check everything, including name, title and address; mistakes are so easily made. I may seem to be labouring the point but I have seen them all.

FROM THE EXPERTS

What should be in a sponsorship proposal?

- ❖ 'I need to understand the guts of the proposal first read-through.'
- ❖ 'I look for value for money.'
- ❖ 'I'm interested in long-term viability.'
- ❖ 'The first thing I ask when I read a proposal is, What can they provide that will enhance my company?'
- ❖ 'Don't tell half the story. I can't make any decision without all the facts.'
- ❖ 'Some seem to think we can read their minds. We don't know them or their organisation, yet they want us to give them money purely on the basis that they asked for it.'
- ❖ 'I refuse to buy a pig in a poke.'

LESSONS TO TAKE FROM THIS CHAPTER

No matter what the format, present your proposal in a logical sequence. The sponsorship manager needs to know:

❖ What is the property on offer?
❖ What support does the organisation want?
❖ What benefit does their company get for its support?

Arouse your reader's awareness, interest and curiosity:

❖ Attract their interest with an eye-catching heading.
❖ Involve them by using 'you' and 'your', 'we' and 'us'.

Make proposals clear and concise:

❖ Ensure that your proposal has every piece of information the decisionmaker will need.
❖ The amount of detail you provide is like salt in a recipe: not enough or too much spoils the meal.

Before posting your letter or pressing 'send', check that:

❖ you have the right name and correct spelling
❖ you have directed the letter to a person, not a department, vague title or 'To whom it may concern'
❖ the position title of the target is correct in every detail
❖ you have verified the address
❖ the right letter is in the right envelope
❖ you have double-checked the above (then rechecked it).

SUGGESTED RESEARCH EXERCISES

1. Read some of your organisation's old sponsorship proposals. Do they follow a logical sequence? With the benefit of this chapter, do you consider them appropriate?
    a. For practice, select one old proposal and rewrite it using what you have learned here. Compare the two.
    b. Now prepare a brief proposal for a target sponsor using the information you have learned so far. Show it to a colleague and ask for feedback.

2. Find out what type of database your organisation is using to record current or potential sponsors' names, titles and addresses and ascertain how long ago it was last updated.
    a. Does it contain all relevant contacts? If not, do you know why?
    b. Select three at random. If any are found to be incorrect,

conduct a complete review of information storage and maintenance.

FURTHER READING

10 essential steps to create a winning sponsorship proposal, http://practicalsponsorshipideas.com/blog/31-create-a-winning-sponsorship-proposal

How Do Sponsors Evaluate Sponsorship Proposals? , http://powersponsorship.com/how-do-sponsors-evaluate-sponsorship-proposals/

MORE MUSINGS FROM THE EXPERTS

- ❖ 'Who is this person asking for my products or money?' That is what I am thinking when I pick up your proposal. Tell me who you are and give me a little background. It is surprising how many organisations omit this important information.'
- ❖ 'Your proposal is not about you and what you want. It is about what you can do for my company.'
- ❖ 'Tell me what you want. Who you are and what you will do with my money are ok, but tell me how much you want. If you don't have this clearly in your proposal then I cannot help you.'

SPONSORSHIP FACT

Sponsorship is not charity or a handout or a simple donation. Sponsorship requires work and the understanding that both partners have to play a role. The sponsorship must benefit the operations of both organisations.

Eleven

The initial interview

'The most important thing in communication is
to hear what isn't being said.'
Peter F. Drucker

Yes! The target has received your proposal and you have been invited
to attend their premises for further discussions. You are about to enter the
plush inner corridors of the maze.

What do you take?

A copy of the proposal

You might need to refer to your proposal during negotiations and,
heaven forbid; the sponsorship manager may have misplaced the original
copy. (It does happen. Remember that desk, piled high with proposals, mail
and event paraphernalia?) If neither of you has a copy, then negotiations will
proceed on a shaky basis filled with 'I think' and 'If . . . then' statements. Or
half the precious meeting time will be wasted as the sponsorship manager
riffles through the contents of their desk or filing cabinet. Hardly ideal. You
want 100 per cent of your time spent in meaningful, fruitful discussion.

Supporting information

Take along anything that will corroborate your claim for a given
amount of sponsorship. This might include budgets, photographs of
facilities, quotes, mock-ups of signs that include the sponsor logo – virtually
anything that intensifies your claim and encourages the sponsorship
manager to look favourably on your property.

A notebook

You will need to take notes of the discussion so that you have a written
record of what was agreed. You may also need to report back to your
committee. Don't rely on your memory because the substance of these

meetings can be complex and the pace rapid. Take a good old fashioned paper and pencil, or an electronic note-taker or android tablet—anything, as long as you have a clear and detailed record of what was discussed.

The right attitude

There is no need to be intimidated by the person you are meeting – remember that it is in their best interests to listen to all you have to say. Accord them the respect you would any other person with whom you hope to do business. They have invited you here, you have their attention, and now is your moment to convey all that a document might not. Your attitude to the proposal is important: if you answer questions in a monosyllabic 'yes' or 'no', even if born of nervousness, you won't advance your cause at all. The person with a passionate belief in the mutual benefits flowing from the proposed relationship will ignite a similar enthusiasm in the listener.

Be on time

Busy people are like the time and tide: they wait for no one. Ensure that you are seated in the outer office or cafe or wherever the meeting is to take place at least five minutes before the scheduled time. You may have to wait for a bit if the person you are meeting with is having a bad day, but that is a small matter when held against the chance you have been given to present your proposal in person.

If the sponsorship manager keeps you waiting for an inordinate length of time, it's poor form. If you keep the sponsorship manager waiting, it's proposal suicide. I know that when, for unavoidable reasons, I kept someone waiting for an appointment, I tried to compensate by giving the proposal slightly more attention than I might otherwise have done.

So plan ahead. If you are meeting in a busy area where parking could prove difficult, build that into your time allowance and set off earlier, or use public transport if your meeting is to take place close to a train station or bus stop. This is a fairly hassle-free option that does not involve unexpected traffic hold-ups, searching for an elusive parking spot or rummaging in the glove box to find coins for the meter. Traffic detours or parking problems are usually reflected in people's faces and may be recognised in their flustered and disoriented manner. If you have had a quiet train ride spent thumbing through the documentation one last time, you are more likely to arrive fresh and ready to perform at your optimum level. Whichever mode of transport you choose, plan ahead.

Dress appropriately for the location

Meetings can be held in quite unexpected and sometimes even unsuitable locations. You would imagine that the sponsorship manager's office would be the obvious venue, but this will not necessarily be the case. The interview might be conducted in an office, but it might also be in a retail outlet, a boardroom, a factory or possibly over a cup of coffee at a cafe.

It may seem breathtakingly obvious, but if you are meeting in a boardroom, don't wear a tropical shirt, red trousers and sneakers (as I have seen happen). Do not wear revealing clothing if you are a woman (I have seen this done also and intentional or not, it is distracting.) If you dress so inappropriately it will be your appearance that leaves the lasting impression, not the material you present. When you meet in a boardroom or office, most of the people you will meet on your way through the building, and certainly the sponsorship manager, will be wearing business clothing. My advice is 'When in Rome . . .' Don't arrive in jeans and T-shirt – you will probably feel uncomfortable and embarrassed and that will be translated into your presentation style. You want to present a professional appearance that says, 'I'm on your wavelength, and we are both professionals ready to do business'.

However, if the meeting is to be held at a restaurant or an event such as a school fete, then a collar, tie and suit would look ludicrously out of place. Allow common sense to prevail and dress according to the situation.

What to do once you're in

You are sitting in the sponsorship manager's reception area, having presented yourself to the department secretary or to the manager's personal assistant (PA). Use your waiting time to sit quietly and go over the main points of the proposal in your mind. The door opens and the sponsorship manager is before you. Don't forget to smile: this person is going to be your friend; they will make your dreams reality and you are going to be of great service to their company. Say 'Thank you for seeing me' as you enter the office. From the moment you shake hands, you are building a relationship. For some the relationship will be a brief one that ends with the meeting; for others it may last for years. Start out as though you are in the latter group.

A rose by any other name . . .

In most cases you will not have actually met before, so a formal greeting is required: Mr. Smith, Ms Jones. The Sponsorship manager will almost certainly ask that you use their given name, but do not do so until invited.

Listen to their preferred name. Mike is not Mick, Mickey or even Michael. Nor is Christine Chris, Chrissie or any other permutation. They have given you their preferred name, so use it. Some people have problems remembering names, especially if they are flustered at the moment of introduction. It's always wise to jot the person's preferred name down on the right-hand top corner of the notepad you are now glad you brought. Even if you feel confident that the name is locked inside your steel trap of a memory ready for instant recall, jot it down anyway. You might have to call the person a few weeks down the track and if your steel trap jams, you will be able to refer to your notes.

It may be that you walk into the meeting room to be faced by a panel of interviewers, there to help the decision maker evaluate your presentation. If you haven't prepared yourself for this eventuality, it can be quite confronting. Here's a tip: draw a quick shape representing the table and jot down the name of each person in their relative position will always be able to address the right person with the correct name. This can be an impressive feat, which will reflect well on you.

Black with one

If you are offered a beverage, accept it graciously whether you want one or not. Although your acceptance displays your good manners and sociability, it is also an opportunity to buy time. Most hosts avoid terminating a conversation while their guest still has coffee in their cup, so the discussions will continue until your cup is empty. Used well, the humble cup of java can actually control the length of the meeting.

This may seem an odd suggestion but it can work. I recall several instances when I had already decided that the deal was not on. I would have concluded the meeting at that point but as the interviewee still had coffee in their cup, I let it continue. On at least two occasions, between my silent negative decision and the last sip of coffee, additional information was introduced that changed my thinking and reversed my decision. Admittedly, this ploy is a long shot, but what do you have to lose?

Impress by being natural

During the interview, don't try to be anything or anyone you are not. Speak in plain English and don't try to impress by using words you don't understand; *never* use words others don't understand. Jargonese is a language best spoken only with the natives of your own land – be it sporting or artistic lingo or indecipherable acronyms. It is insider talk that alienates everyone else. If you don't understand a point being made or a term used, ask for clarification. Don't be embarrassed. It's far better to ask at this point than to find you have agreed to something totally unacceptable through a misunderstanding. If you nod intelligently, the interviewer has every right to think you have understood. You can prepare yourself by studying some of the sponsorship terms used in this book and in the articles that appear at the end of each chapter and in the recommended further readings.

Research shows that standard social exchange is a complex business, with only 7 per cent of communication expressed verbally. Eyes are important tools of communication, our 'windows to the soul'. Aristotle Onassis, the late shipping magnate, always wore dark glasses while negotiating so as not to expose his stance and spoil his chances of securing the best deal. Unless your target dons dark glasses a` la Onassis, look them in the eye. You have nothing to hide; you are going to be honest, open and forthright, so communicate that through your willingness to make eye contact.

Keep the eye contact steady, though not intimidating. When someone's eyes dart all over the place or stare fixedly at the floor or at a point just over our left shoulder, we tend to wonder what they are hiding. Are they uncertain of their subject, nervous, shifty or just plain rude? Another reason for maintaining good eye contact is that you can more accurately gauge a person's level of involvement in the conversation. When the pupils dilate it is a sign that you have hit a topic that arouses interest. Use that. Expand on this point and engage them more fully in the project as a whole.

External distractions

As stated, it is vital that you have your target's undivided attention. You have your fifteen minutes of fame and you want them free of distraction. The location of the meeting will determine the number of outside distractions you can expect and the degree to which they will interrupt your negotiations. When time is tight and negotiations delicate, the concentration factor is critical for both you and your target.

Ideally a meeting should be held at your premises, where you can control the level and frequency of interruptions. This ideal is rarely achieved because you are not in a position to make such a demand. Invariably, you must go where the money is. I would estimate that in periods of relative calm I found it necessary to attend external meetings only about 5 per cent of the time. In an office you can expect phones to ring, secretaries to interrupt, and the target's colleagues to need urgent access to them. You have no power in this situation, but you can compensate by using the rewinding technique set out below. Sometimes an office, with all its attendant distractions, is preferable to a cafe or similar. There you sit, driving home a winning point, the sponsorship manager's eyes are dilating, you are truly in control and your target is mesmerised,

body language screaming 'I'm interested, give me more . . .', when the waiter appears at your side and asks to take your order. Bang. The moment is gone and the target's concentration has shifted completely to the absorbing question of 'latte or long black?' While they regard the menu and its gastronomic offerings with the kind of slavering relish you had hoped to engender by your presentation, you must patiently grind your teeth and wait for the next break between ordering, order arriving, wiping spills off your once-pristine pages and the inevitable 'Will there be anything else?' from your attentive waiter.

Don't become flustered and question the parentage of the café staff, who are just doing their job. Do yours. Accept that in a noisy and animated environment it is impossible to keep your target's attention throughout. It is up to you to repair the damage and put the temporarily derailed meeting back on track.

On a personal note, I love having coffee outside of the office environment with new people, and I do it at every opportunity. I find that on one hand I am more relaxed, while on the other more receptive and attentive to what is being said to me. Might be the caffeine buzz, but I only attend these meetings if I believe that they will be productive. My time is valuable so I will expect you to be concise and expressive what you are seeking, what makes you different to your competitors, and the reasons why I should support you.

Rewinding

Wait until the waiter leaves and, just like a tape deck, rewind the conversation to the point not at, but just prior to, the interruption, so that the target is reminded of the details leading up to the moment of distraction and loses none of the important points you've made. This repairs the break in the conversation's flow. Depending on where you are and the degree of interference, you may have to employ the rewind technique many times. It takes patience and practice, but it is a skill that, once mastered, will enable you to keep control of the interview.

Commit the rewind technique to memory and practice it. If you feel confident in its use, the distraction, however badly timed, will not cause you the heartache it might have. You can use the target's time of agony ('Which coffee, and should I have cake?') to regain your composure and mentally revisit the last couple of minutes, choosing a point at which to recommence. When you have regained attention, recap the major points so far and pick up the conversation a few steps back from where you were when interrupted.

We request the pleasure . . .

At some time during the meeting, invite the sponsorship manager to attend one of your events as a guest of your organisation. It is always easier to negotiate on your home ground, especially if all your members are there to support you and make the sponsorship manager feel welcome. A picture is worth a thousand words and possibly even more dollars, and no matter how eloquent your description, the sponsorship manager will find first-hand evidence of your claims far more compelling.

The end of the interview

When your meeting has proved successful and terms and negotiations have been agreed upon, my advice – and I say this with all respect – is to shut up. It is easy to get carried away with the euphoria of the occasion and start to make extra promises that you can't really deliver. It happens. On occasions I have had to duck to avoid all the extras being thrown at me – benefits that were not mentioned during the negotiations. Why do it? You have secured your deal, your negotiated benefits have been accepted, your sponsor is happy – there is nothing more to add. There are three excellent reasons for stopping here:
- ❖ Your sponsor has already negotiated a price and will not add any more for your extra benefits – benefits that you may be able to package and sell to another target sponsor.
- ❖ If you start adding sweeteners your sponsor might begin to wonder if you have been holding out on them during negotiations. Do not let

the seeds of mistrust germinate; you haven't even signed a contract at this   stage, so don't give the sponsor any reason to reconsider.

❖ You might want to consider adding these extras as surprise bonuses during the life of the contract as goodwill gestures that will be noted at renegotiation time. You may deeply regret anything you now say in haste.

Simply say what the next step will be and wind things up.

Thank the sponsorship manager for the chance or opportunity to present your case and for their valuable time. This is a 'mere' courtesy but it will be appreciated.

Then:
❖ Ask how long it will take for them to make a decision if one has not already been reached, and say that you will call on that day. (This pins them down to a time frame. It also signals that you are on the ball and keen to follow up on what was discussed.)

❖ Ask if any further information is required that will help in the decision-making process. (This shows that you are offering to put all and any information and material at their disposal and demonstrates that your organisation and its processes are open to, and unafraid of, any scrutiny.)

❖ Arrange a day for the sponsorship manager to attend one of your events, and schedule it prior to the date on which they will make their decision about your proposal.

❖ Go out and shout yourself a beer or a chardonnay or a latte (or will that be a long black?).

A final word of advice on the interview: no matter what the outcome of your meeting might be, always leave on good terms. If you have been unsuccessful this time, there is always another time. A former boss once gave me some good advice: 'The wheels turn, son.' Situations and circumstances change, positions can reverse. Always leave the door open because you never know when another opportunity will arise and you may need the goodwill you have created.

As you leave the outer office, thank the secretary or personal assistant for their help. It is more than likely that this person was your first contact, that they helped set up the meeting, and that, if your proposal is successful, you will deal with them again.

LESSONS TO TAKE FROM THIS CHAPTER

- Take all relevant backup material to the interview – and don't forget your copy of the proposal.
- Be punctual.
- Allow plenty of time to arrive cool, calm and with everything collected.
- Dress appropriately.
- Remember names.
- Drink the coffee (slowly).
- Use eye contact.
- An interruption-free meeting is a rare thing, so accept interruptions gracefully
- Employ the rewind technique as necessary, and keep control.
- Invite the sponsorship manager to visit one of your organisation's events.
- Stick to your game plan and don't make rash offers.
- Leave on good terms no matter what the outcome.

SUGGESTED RESEARCH EXERCISES

1.   It is said that first impressions are lasting impressions; we apparently sum up a person within thirty seconds of meeting them.
    a.   What sort of first impression do you make?
    b.   Ask some honest friends and colleagues to tell you what their first impressions of you were.
    c.   What can you do to change any negative reactions?
2.   To help you with that rewind technique, next time you are having a conversation in a place where there is a lot of noise or action – a party, a bar, the football – count the number of times your conversation is interrupted. Each time you are the one who is interrupted, employ the rewind technique:
    a.   Wait until the distraction ceases, roll the conversation back to a little before the interruption and start there.
    b.   Does your companion keep up with the gist of the conversation?
    c.   Do they fully comprehend what you said?
    d.   To find out, ask them later, in a quieter place, to recount some of the details of what you said.
3.   Prepare for a meeting with an imaginary target sponsor. Set a day, place and time for this meeting and get ready, as though you must leave the house or office at a certain time to reach the meeting on time. When you believe you are ready, do a check. Look in the mirror. Could you describe yourself as well groomed?

Now check your briefcase or bag.

- ❖ Do you have all the necessary documents?
- ❖ Do you have pens and perhaps a calculator or your tablet to take electronic notes?
- ❖ Do you have change for a parking meter if you are driving?

A SPONSORSHIP MANAGER'S PERSPECTIVE ON MAKING THE CALL

'Some of the most frequently asked questions amongst new sponsor seekers pertains to the process for making initial contact with a potential sponsor. Should a phone call be placed first? When do you send the proposal? Should you have a meeting with the prospect? Do you have to make a presentation? The answer to any of these questions really depends on the circumstances surrounding the request. Situational factors such as the targeted company's sponsorship policy, the relationship (or lack thereof) that you have with the company, whether or not you have access to company employees and the amount of information you have about the company all contribute to the process you follow in making initial contact with a potential sponsor.'

FROM THE EXPERTS

'The greatest difficulty with making the initial call is getting the right person on the phone.'

'If you are successful in landing an initial meeting learn as much as possible while you talk to them.'

'When calling a prospective sponsor for the first time, you should try to use inside influence, if it exists.'

'When you are in a meeting, make sure you have defined objective, that you volunteer information about your organization and you gather every bit of information about the sponsor and their objectives.'

FURTHER READING

Hyatt, M., (2012), *Platform: Get Noticed in a Noisy World*, Thomas Nelson.

Dealing With Distractions and Interruptions: Strategies for Staying Focused on Important Tasks,
http://www.theproductivitypro.com/FeaturedArticles/article00144.htm

Smith, J., (2001), Handling Effective Meetings - What You Need to Know: Definitions, Best Practices, Benefits and Practical Solutions, Tebbo Publishing

A WORD ON COFFEE MEETINGS FROM THE EXPERTS

❖ 'I don't care who pays, it is not a problem for me if the sponsorship seeker grabs the check. It is not that a sponsorship can be bought for the price of a cup of coffee.'
❖ 'I feel that someone in a position of power (the sponsorship manager) should not allow anyone who wants something from him to buy him anything - even a coffee.'
❖ 'If I have been asked to attend the meeting, then they should pay. If I have requested them to meet me for coffee and a discussion then I will pay. Either way, I always carry my wallet to cover either scenario.'

SPONSORSHIP FACT

Proposals must indicate the benefits of the property to the sponsor and how they meet the sponsor's objectives.

Twelve

Drawing up a contract

'An oral contract isn't worth the paper
it's written on.'
SAMUEL GOLDWYN

You have built a good relationship with your sponsor, and the manager with whom you are dealing seems to be an honest individual who has no reason to withhold anything that has been promised. Likewise, you are a person of integrity and will deliver all that you have agreed in return for the sponsorship. A simple handshake between two mature, honest parties confident of each other's intentions and abilities should be sufficient then. Or perhaps not.

In my survey, managers said they sought written agreements for arrangements that were expected to cover periods of more than six months. They did this to protect both the sponsor and the event or property. Some of them cited problems that had arisen that would have been catastrophic had binding agreements not been firmly in place. Most managers thought that they needed a contract listing all the benefits they expected to receive in order to be sure of receiving them. Many quoted cases where past non-contractual arrangements had gone amiss, at considerable costs in finance and resources to the company for nil return. A minority (mostly from small firms) said that to sponsor a one-off event they would not insist on a contract as the risks were minimal.

Why have a written contract?

Why would a verbal contract agreed on by all parties become a matter for dispute? Consider the following scenarios:
- ❖ One of the parties has interpreted the agreement differently.
- ❖ There is a serious breach of the agreement.
- ❖ There is a falling-out between the parties on a business or personal level.
- ❖ One party leaves their organisation and there are no legal records of the agreement.
- ❖ One party is knocked down by a bus tomorrow.

Intentions always appear pure and clear at the outset and everyone certainly intends to conform to the word and the spirit of the agreement, but should the unexpected occur then those intentions may become subject to the determination of a judge. Believe me, the handshake agreement of today can result in heartache tomorrow. We are all familiar with the court cases that arose from grievances over contractual disagreements. When one party feels wronged – even when legal documentation exists – a messy court battle can ensue.

A clearly written contract, duly signed and witnessed, provides you with a much firmer footing on which to argue your case should the necessity arise. It is a document that spells out all the terms and conditions of the sponsorship, detailing the rights and obligations of all signatories. It is a safeguard for all parties and is sensible business practice.

What is in a contract?

Put simply, a contract is an agreement by two or more parties to create rights and obligations that are enforceable by law. We enter into a contract to clarify the basis on which we are legally bound by the promises we make. In order to be legally enforceable, a contract must contain six elements:

1. Intention

All parties must have had the intention to create a legal relationship. (Our organisation wants to be sponsored by company Y and company Y wants to sponsor us, and both parties intend their agreement to have legal force.)

2. Offer and acceptance

One party must make an offer and the other party must accept it, so that there is clear agreement between the parties.

3. Consideration

Consideration is the price to be paid for a promise before the promise is legally enforceable. (You will give us the agreed sponsorship fee and, in exchange, we will give you sole-category sponsorship rights; that is, your brands will be the only products in that category sold at our events. If your product is chocolate, then no rival chocolates will be sold.)

4. Legal capacity

Both parties must have the legal capacity to enter into the agreement. The usual list of those without capacity includes minors and, under certain conditions, mentally unsound and intoxicated people.

5. Consent

Genuine consent of both parties must be given for the contract to be valid. Neither party can be forced into signing.

6. Legality

The agreement must be legal: any contracts entered into for illegal purposes are of no effect. Occasionally you read about a million-dollar deal that was recorded on a paper napkin, and in fact so long as the six elements listed above are covered and the intention is clear, then a paper napkin is as good as a legal document. Such a seemingly casual record is, however, really for those who have played the game many times and who are extremely canny even when using a thumbnail dipped in tar. Most of us are better served with a more formal and well-considered approach.

What details to include

You may feel that you do not have the expertise, knowledge, skill or experience needed to draw up a binding contract, and your organisation may not have the funds to hire a solicitor. Yet a basic contract is a fairly simple document that most of us, with some thought and care, can design and write. It is best to type up your way. The major elements you will need to include are:

❖ the names of the parties entering the agreement, that is, the sponsor (individual or corporate) and the sponsored party (organisation or individual)
❖ the dates on which the agreement starts and finishes
❖ the benefits that the sponsor will receive under the agreement
❖ when the sponsor will receive such benefits
❖ the fee or payment to which the sponsor has agreed
❖ when the fee will be paid
❖ if there is to be an option to renew the contract, which party has the option
❖ dated signatures of authorised people from each organisation

- dated signatures of witnesses to the signing of the agreement
- the annual rate of increase for the sponsorship fee expressed in percentages, when it will be paid and how
- full details of exclusivity arrangements
- details of the initial fee payment, when it will be paid and how
- full details of any performance-based fee payments, how the performance will be monitored and how the incentive works*
- your authority to use your sponsor's logos and trademarks, all restrictions and requirements for their use, including artwork and design approval
- a clear statement detailing those terms and areas that you do not want included in the contract. (For example, high-profile people may not want photos of their families to be used by sponsors for commercial purposes. They would therefore insert a clause in the contract that would prohibit this without written permission.)

*

I can only recall ever entering into one performance-based contract. It was with a football club whose president was a bookmaker who liked to add the element of risk to his agreements. His club was paid a base sponsorship fee and would receive further progressive payments should the team reach the finals, win through to the Grand Final playoff and ultimately win. The team achieved success, winning the Grand Final and in the process adding three additional incentive payments to the coffers. I later heard that similar deals had been struck with other sponsors, resulting in a windfall for the club. The promise of additional payments had been used as an incentive to the players to play above expectations.)

In the 'showbag of samples' section that has been included at the back of this book you will find an example of a simple contract between a fictitious sponsoring firm and an imaginary organisation seeking sponsorship. It is a simple format that will suffice in most circumstances. Get into the habit of using this format (adjusted to fit your particular needs and circumstances), as it may prove a vital protection for your organisation should a dispute occur.

The duration of a sponsorship agreement

What is the ideal duration? The length of any agreement depends on the situation and circumstances that surround it. Your viewpoint will also colour the answer. From the sponsor's point of view, the ideal time would be the exact period it takes to achieve whatever goal they are aiming for by using the property. For the sponsored organisation, an indefinite period stretching well beyond the foreseeable future seems about right.

Most agreements have a clearly defined expiry date and, if not simply covering a single event, will usually endure for one, two, three or five years. Most of the contracts I negotiated were for either three- or five-year periods. In general, I avoided one-year agreements for these reasons: firstly, I believe that a sponsor does not really start to feel the benefits of an association until at least the second year, and secondly, there is rarely a return on your investment first time round.

In my survey, most sponsorship managers agreed that three years seems an optimal period. They said that this allows for the development of a strong relationship, marketplace identification of that relationship and a return on initial investment. The first year of a sponsorship contract is one where all parties are trying each other out. I used the first year to work out all the ways I could use a property to my company's advantage, and to begin developing relationships with the relevant event managers. The sponsor usually makes their biggest investment in year one as they build on the sponsorship. For example, they need to pay for extra advertising to ensure that target consumers and the world at large are quickly made aware of the company's involvement in the event. A general rule of thumb is to invest 50 cents in promotion for every dollar committed to a sponsorship. Should a company pay $100 000 for sponsorship rights it is most likely that an additional $50 000 will be spent in year one to support their position as sponsor. The payback from this investment must then come in the contract's remaining years.

A word of warning about long-term agreements. A three-year sponsorship may seem very appealing at first, but remember you will be bound by it for that full period. Your attitude when accepting the terms of a sponsorship agreement must be that all other sponsors in that category are off-limits until the contract expires. My advice is to sign only short-term deals if you do not have the fortitude to go the distance or if you want the freedom to accept a better offer at the end of twelve months. Should another sponsor come courting, talk to them and place them on the bottom tier of your hierarchy – the one for potential sponsors. Keep them in this position and at arm's length until the day your existing sponsorship agreement expires. At that time you and your sponsor are generally free of all obligations to each other and can enter agreements with whomever you like. Until that time, morally and legally you can have no contract with your 'sponsor in the wings'.

Seeking clarity and avoiding mistakes

Having the agreement in writing is helpful and wise, but even before the ink is dry there can be a problem. One party thinks a certain issue covered is black under the terms of the agreement while the other is just as certain that it is white. It happens more often than you would think and I have found myself in this predicament on a couple of occasions. This situation has a name under contract law, one that is uncharacteristically clear: it is called a mistake. A mistake will not necessarily prevent the formation of a contract or limit its operation, but a party may be able to avoid some of the consequences of the mistake. Rather than become too involved in contract law, I will just say that there are legal remedies for mistakes, but why risk an unfavourable outcome? Avoid making them in the first place. Insist that the contract be drawn up in plain English and take legal advice if you think there are any tricky clauses.

I always enjoy watching the Marx Brothers' 1935 movie A Night at the Opera, in which Groucho Marx is attempting to explain the intricacies of a rather dubious business contract to Chico Marx. When Groucho mentions the Sanity Clause, Chico responds, "You can't fool me. There ain't no Santy Clause!" Don't allow your contracts to become elaborate mysteries: equally, don't allow them to read like a Marx brother's script. Protect yourself and your sponsors by producing a clear and unambiguously worded document. The law is on your side.

You can be assured that most sponsors will have the resources to engage lawyers to provide advice on sponsorship agreements. I would often seek legal advice to avoid ambiguity in contracts and to ensure that my company's interests were protected. Be advised: do likewise. Should you have any doubts, seek legal advice. It might seem a costly exercise, but in the long term, should a problem arise, it will have been a wise decision.

Frustrated and broken – contracts and relationships

There are two major causes of disputes over sponsorship contracts:
- Frustrated contracts, where an unexpected event occurs over which neither party has any control and which makes performance of the contract impossible: for example, two days before your sponsored event a cyclone hits, carrying away your venue and all its trappings.
- Breached contracts, where one of the parties fails to perform as agreed and therefore breaches the terms of the contract: for

example, you promise your sponsor sole category rights but then allow a competitor in.

Even though a contract is discharged from the moment the frustrating event occurs, the contract still remains valid up until this time. The rights that have occurred before the event may still be enforceable. Where an amount has been paid for performance under a contract, but no performance has occurred, a party may be entitled to be reimbursed; in other words, an advance of sponsorship monies may have to be repaid.

It is a basic principle of contract law that parties should keep their promises. Where one party has breached the contract, the innocent party may be entitled to treat the agreement as finished and sue for damages. This unpleasant circumstance does occur in sponsorship agreements from time to time. Some organisations are happy to take a sponsor's money and agree to terms at the outset, but when a charming competitor with a seductive line, and possibly a better offer, comes calling, they may set aside their scruples and enter into a liaison with the new sponsor in an arrangement that is entirely contrary to the existing contract.

I have experienced this situation and have taken the hard line. One such case occurred during a time of heavy competitive effort when a rival was approaching our sponsorship properties, apparently enticing them to enter into new sponsorship arrangements. Most replied with a polite and correct 'thanks but no thanks', but there will always be a few that can't resist. One morning, the representative of a property with whom I had a good relationship approached me with a simple and direct demand. His organisation had been approached by our rival and offered $60,000 over three years. If we didn't match it, he had been authorised to terminate our existing contract. Our current deal included a fee of $3,500 a year for three years. Tucked safely in my filing cabinet was a contract with two years left to run which included an option for a further three years, and that option was held by my company. I politely registered my disappointment and informed this person that I would instigate immediate legal action.

Certainly the other offer was better, but tough luck. A contract is a contract and the law was firmly on our side. I chose not to treat the particular contract as finished and sue for damages because I believed this sponsorship to be strategically worthwhile. Instead, I sought an injunction to stop the club from accepting the competitor's offer.

Twenty-four hours before the matter was to go before the court, the sponsored organisation rang me with the news that its board had decided to honour the existing contract.

A great deal of work on both sides went into restoring the damaged relationship, but such cases leave a sour aftertaste that can linger for a long time. It is a warning about the potential problems inherent in long-term agreements. This organisation's representatives had found the prospect of a three-year sponsorship very appealing at the time, but much less attractive when they found they were stuck in it with no legal way out.

Beware the Trade Practices Act

In the USA the law of unfair competition is mainly governed by state common law. Federal law may apply in the areas of trademarks, copyrights, and false advertising. The EU has the Unfair Commercial Practices Directive while Australia has the Trade Practices Act (TPA) and the various state and territory Fair Trading Act equivalents which have all affected the traditional rules of contract. In Australia, (and here I will discuss the Australian context), the TPA prohibits misleading and deceptive conduct in commercial relations, and also the making of certain contracts that involve restrictive practices.

While we are discussing exclusive category sponsors, a word regarding 'third line forcing' in the TPA. This occurs where you supply goods or services to a party on the condition that they acquire other goods or services from another supplier specified by you. If you are considering appointing a caterer or other supplier to service your events, take great care.

In your contract your sponsor will often insert a clause which demands that only their products be available at the event, and you will naturally expect your caterer to sell your sponsor's products exclusively. Such a clause may contravene section 47 of the TPA, which prohibits 'exclusive dealing'. The caterer is disadvantaged by being forced to buy from the sponsor on the sponsor's terms.

As an example of the response of the Trade Practices Commission or TPC (now the Australian Competition and Consumer Commission or ACCC) to third line forcing, consider the case of *TPC v. Legion Cabs (Trading) Co-operative Society Ltd* (1978) ATPR 40- 092. The TPC took action against Legion Cabs for requiring its members to purchase a quota of petrol from Shell. Those who did not comply were charged higher fees for their radio service. The Federal Court fined Legion Cabs $3000, saying that the company had contravened section 47 of the Trade Practices Act.

Most companies are well aware of this legislation and get around it by doing a side deal with the caterer. The sponsoring company simply enters into an agreement with the caterer. Here the consideration is again the sale or use of the sponsor's products in return for cash, products or logistical support. For example, at CUB we would often provide caterers with equipment which would lower their operating costs and help them to dispense products more efficiently. You must be careful that you don't get caught when you negotiate your deals with smaller sponsors who might not be aware of the ramifications of third line forcing or other provisions of the TPA.

FROM THE EXPERTS

Do you insist on a binding contract for all your sponsorships? If so, why?

A resounding 'Yes'.

- 'All of our sponsorships are protected by signed contracts.'
- 'If a [no-contract] deal blew up in my face, it would mean my job and career. I'm not taking any chances.'
- 'I had to pick up this position from someone who left it unexpectedly. I would not have known where my company stood if not for a filing cabinet full of contracts.'
- 'No contract – no deal.'
- '[The contract] ensures that both parties have a clear understanding of their rights and obligations to each other.'

What is the preferred length of time (in years) for an agreement to run?

- 'I don't see any value in sponsoring past three years. Priorities change in that time.'
- 'I sometimes sponsor for twelve months and take an option for another two years. That gives me the opportunity to test the water, as it were.'
- 'A short period (twelve months) doesn't give you ownership of a property. Consumers don't really recognise bona fide involvement until year two or three.'

LESSONS TO TAKE FROM THIS CHAPTER

- ❖ The value of signed contracts cannot be overstated.
- ❖ Make sure your contracts are clear and understandable.
- ❖ Take every care to avoid mistakes – never assume the parties understand each other when preparing a contract.
- ❖ If you sign a contract, be prepared to honour it.
- ❖ Remember the Trade Practices Act or similar legislation that is enacted in your country.

SUGGESTED RESEARCH EXERCISES

Look at all your existing sponsorship agreements.
- ❖ How many are signed and binding contracts?
- ❖ How many were handshake deals?
- ❖ Why is there a difference?
- ❖ Have you had any problems with any of these agreements?
- ❖ What was the outcome?

If you have had handshake deals, use the contract format in the 'showbag of samples' section at the back of this book to draw up contracts with those sponsors. Do you think you could talk them into signing the contract? Try one or two.

FURTHER READING

Sponsorship contracts have to protect reputations of both parties, http://www.independent.ie/business/media/sponsorship-contracts-have-to-protect-reputations-of-both-parties-29850622.html

http://www.simpsons.com.au/wp-content/uploads/chapter-21-sponsorship.pdf

http://www.acc.com/legalresources/publications/topten/sla.cfm

SPONSORSHIP THOUGHT

Morality clauses are now becoming 'must haves' in sponsorship contracts. The clauses are in essence get out clause that allows either party to terminate should one party tarnish their image or bring negative publicity upon themselves or the sponsor. Recent high profile examples of sports stars losing sponsorship over reputational damage include Tiger Woods, Wayne Rooney, Lance Armstrong, Ian Thorpe and Oscar Pretorius.

SPONSORSHIP FACT

In acquiring sponsorship rights, 47 percent of UK sponsors said that they would spend more for the period 2014—2015. Of that percentage, three percent said that their spending would "increase substantially".

Thirteen

Keeping your sponsors

'Coming together is a beginning, staying together
is progress and working together is success.'
HENRY FORD

Wise words, Henry, and just the quote to lead us into a discussion of
how to keep your partnership a success. You and your sponsors have
signed on the dotted line and the sponsorship fee is in the bank, as good
as spent. But how will you ensure that you keep the sponsor's patronage?
You must never give them cause to doubt the wisdom of their decision;
in fact, they should bask in the comforting notion that it was a decision
made of sound judgement.

A commitment to each other

When I asked my survey respondents, 'What do you expect from your
sponsorship partners in return for your support?', all agreed that they
expected their partners to provide the benefits and opportunities as set
out in the contracted agreements. There were stories of organisations that
were happy to 'take the money and run', and even of properties that went
into agreements knowing they would be unable to provide all they
promised. Others signed virtually the same agreement with several
sponsors, which meant that no sponsor was adequately provided for.
Interestingly, most managers felt that these scenarios resulted more from
unprofessional conduct or lack of understanding or experience than from
blatant dishonesty.

I suggest that while you and your sponsor are together, you should
each treat your relationship with the commitment of a marriage and work
hard to make it a success. One of the major reasons cited for marriage
breakdowns is that, over time, couples take each other for granted. This
can never be allowed to happen in your relationship with your sponsors.
You have made a serious commitment and you should see that nothing

stops you from honouring every clause of the agreement up to the minute it expires. In the initial period of euphoria it all seems pretty easy, but there will be times of stress when you will need help to Prevail against the forces that seek to separate you from your word. Back to Henry's quote above.

'Coming together is a beginning . . .'

I have no argument with this statement. At the beginning you have not yet had the chance to demonstrate to your sponsor that you will perform as promised. Neither have you shown an unwillingness to do so.

Likewise, the sponsor has not had the time or opportunity to decide whether their decision was right.

'. . . staying together is progress . . .'

The Macquarie Concise Dictionary defines the word 'progress' as 'advancement in general' and 'growth and development; continuous improvement'. These terms are relevant throughout the entire life of the contract. Your aims should be to move forward and improve the quality of life and business for your organisation and your sponsors. As you progress through the contract, you will begin to understand each other more fully, gaining trust and mutual respect while building what will hopefully be a long-term alliance. To this end, each party should make the other aware of any changing circumstances or new factors – harmful or enhancing – that may affect the relationship. No surprises – keep each other informed.

'. . . working together is success'

Build a relationship that works for the advancement and improvement of both parties. You are, after all, working in tandem to improve the position of both organisations in their sectors, and each gains when one flourishes. To ensure mutual success, be aware of the stages in each of the relationship ladder (see Figure 13.1).

Sponsors rule – OK!

No matter how large a sponsor's input, or how small, all sponsors want to be treated as special. Their differing financial contributions and hierarchical positions are relative. Some sponsors will make a large contribution because they can afford it; some will give much less because they have less to invest. Either way, and at all levels, sponsors must be regarded as royalty, and must be made to feel like royalty.

Live by the eight great sponsorship commandments

1. You shall make absolutely sure that during the period of the agreement you give your sponsor all of the promised benefits, in full and to the letter.

2. You shall be cooperative and willing at all times.

3. You shall add to all contracted benefits some unexpected advantages that will surprise and delight the sponsor.

4. You shall prove to your sponsor the benefits of supporting you by preparing regular reports containing figures such as increased sales of their products and media coverage.

5. You shall nurture and maintain a philosophy throughout your organisation that the sponsor is royalty.

6. You shall ensure that your relationship with your sponsor is built on a firm foundation of mutual trust and understanding.

7. You shall make sure that your sponsor is given opportunities to sample your organisation's offerings.

8. You shall never give your sponsor any reason to regret the investment in you or your organisation

Figure 13.1: The relationship ladder

We have developed a balanced, trusting relationship based on mutual respect and loyalty. At this stage the relationship is strong enough to survive major threats and assaults from internal and external influences.

We both add value to each other's organisation and recognise the contribution our relationship represents.

Our friendship blossoms. We commence bonding as a result of the close relationship that is evolving.

As our relationship develops we start to build trust in and respect for each other.

Following successful negotiations we make a firm commitment and begin the 'understanding' process.

Our first tentative steps are to make initial contact and begin negotiation.

We start out as individuals, each wanting to build a successful relationship. This is achieved through a climb (over time) up the relationship ladder where we strive for a mutually rewarding relationship.

START

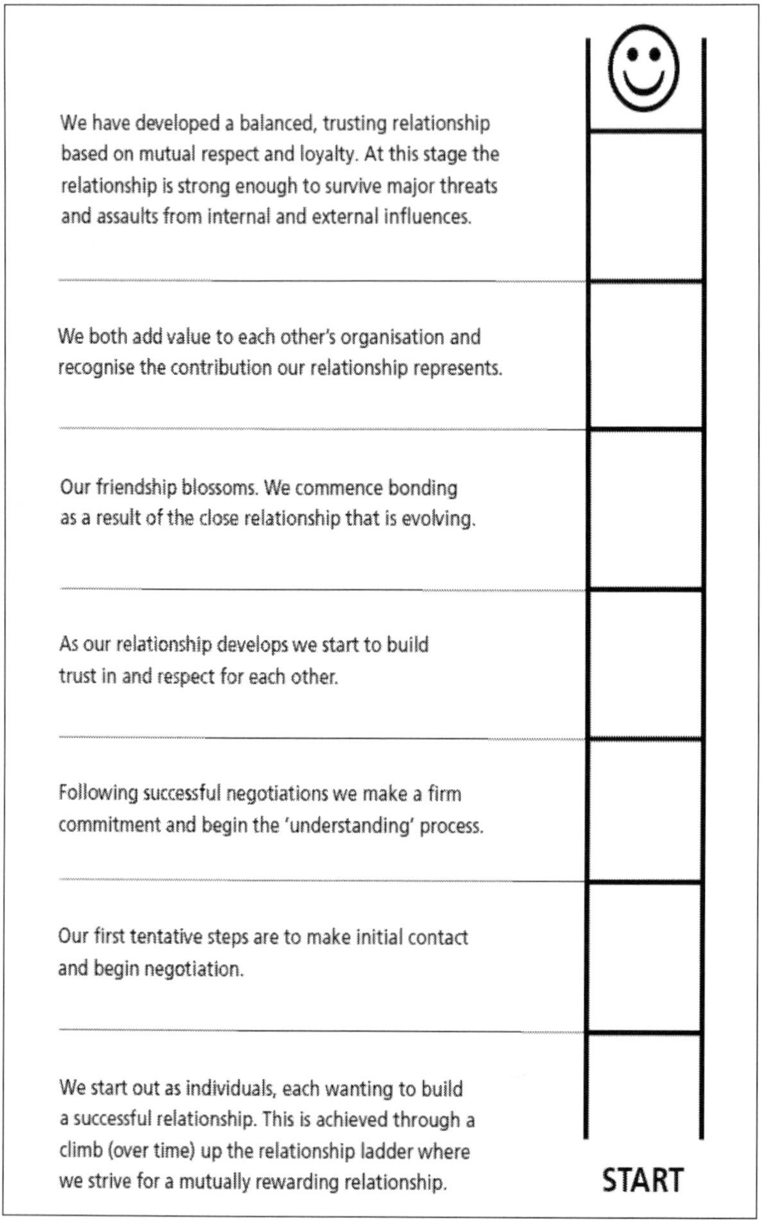

The importance of sponsor recognition:
the Alf Browne plaque story

A sponsorship manager's office walls testify to the gratitude of sponsored individuals and organisations. Every spare centimeter of space will be adorned with photos, plaques and certificates sent as thanks and recognition. Such positive and daily feedback makes for a pleasant work environment.

One particular day, Alf Browne, who was the organiser of the Returned and Services League, Anzac Day race meeting in the country town of Seymour, paid me a visit. His annual trek to my office was more a pleasant formality than a necessity; my company had staunchly supported RSL activities for years and our association with this well-organised event was one we had never regretted. On this occasion, Alf dug into his bag and produced a plaque recognising our support over many years. He said, 'Here, Mike, this is to put up on your brag walls. I got the idea from all the other bits and pieces that I noticed on your walls during previous visits.' He waved his arms expansively to include all the 'brag' material.

I had not thought about it too much before and I acknowledged that, yes, my counterparts and I liked to get these mementos for our offices. The walls of the late E. J. Whitten's office at Adidas were plastered with photos and paraphernalia from sponsored clubs and individuals. Likewise, the obliging John Forbes at Puma had an office reminiscent of a mini sports gallery.

Alf then said something that gave me a new perspective, one that has remained with me. He believed that the fact that we surrounded ourselves with this material was evidence that we were proud of our association with those we sponsored. 'It is also an opportunity,' he said, 'for sponsored people and clubs to have a continuing presence in your company's daily life.'

Think about that. It is simple, but brilliant. It's not hard to organise, nor is it an expensive exercise. It can be a fancy plaque or a simple computer-generated certificate – it doesn't matter so long as it reminds the sponsor of your organisation. Of course, your citation will not be polished and admired every day, but at an unconscious level it will keep you in the sponsor's mind.

Going the extra mile

One of our greatest gifts, one that no one can take from us, is our imagination. You have one and so do I, but how often do we exercise it? Here is the perfect time to give it a decent work-out.

Use your imagination to benefit the position of your sponsor and, by extension, your organisation. Be creative and innovative. Think carefully about what experiences you might give your sponsor and think outside the square. Be inventive and don't discount any idea that presents itself. Unfetter your imagination. Sooner or later you will arrive at a unique solution and set your organisation apart from the pack with its simple genius.

Look at novel ways of involving your sponsor; something different that the sponsor may not have had the chance to participate in had it not been for you.

Two examples from my own experience stand out. One, I was invited to pitch the first ball at the opening game when a baseball centre was officially opened at Altona in Melbourne, and two, I experienced the start of a harness race while seated in the mobile barrier. The horses were snorting and charged up ready to race. As the mobile stated to role we could feel the adrenaline building in the highly strung animals. It was an experience that money could not buy.

Be prepared to give a little extra. Take the plaque example. Why not arrange a small function around the presentation of some such recognition? Or perhaps present it at an event where a crowd of people will see how much you appreciate your sponsor. Such a tactic may sound corny and contrived but it is all part of the game. Remember, we are human beings who have egos and we all like them stroked. One idea that fills several needs simultaneously, including ego-stroking, is the formation of a 'brains trust'. Everyone likes to be considered an expert. Call your sponsors together and tell them you would like to form a 'brains trust' or 'think tank' of fertile minds to generate innovative ideas for your organisation. This not only compliments the sponsor but also draws them further into the life of your organisation, heightens their interest in your success, and broadens your pool of expertise – and, of course, new possibilities evolve from the ideas so generated. Time permitting, I sat on and contributed to many of these 'think tanks.' The ideas and strategies generated often morphed struggling organisations into professional and innovative units. All achieved at no cost and because they invited their sponsors to be involved.

Beware of influential friends

You may initially find it easy to use a friend in a senior position within a company to secure funding. Some influential company people may enter into sponsorship agreements not from commercial consideration but purely from ego, because they:

- ❖ crave personal recognition and exposure, want to rub shoulders with the 'elite' or improve their personal profile with a powerful person from the sponsored company or another sponsor
- ❖ want to be seen as a 'white knight' and have their ego stroked by grateful recipients
- ❖ have a personal reason such as family ties to the sponsored property, or want to impress friends by sponsoring the friends' properties
- ❖ love the 'buzz' of being able to commit company funds to the property of their choice.

In many instances, no real benefits flow back to the company from these often extravagant investments of company money. There is not a lot that a sponsorship manager can do in a situation like this. It's up to the boss . . . until a higher authority or the shareholders query the expense.

If you are the beneficiary of a managing director's whim, great – so long as your benefactor remains in this position of influence. But what if they move on, leaving you and your sponsorship needs behind? It can happen. It does happen. And should the unthinkable occur, the ex-managing director's whims are often the first to be jettisoned.

Be advised: ensure that your relationship with the company is not limited to that one person, however powerful. They will have passed the edict down to their minions to implement, and these 'lesser mortals' are the people you will deal with in the event of your patron moving on. Worse still, the deal you make with the managing director might be of the handshake variety over a glass of fine wine at their exclusive club.

Handshakes will have little currency, however, when the other party is no longer in the relevant position of power.

Make sure you seek out the significant players and start to build a meaningful relationship with them. Do this by asking your patron to introduce you to the company's sponsorship people. Your patron may baulk at this and tell you that you can deal directly with him or her as he or she is personally administering the property. Be polite but insistent. Say that you feel it is matter of courtesy that you at least meet the sponsorship personnel. Once you have met the team and can put names to faces, keep these people informed about the agreement and everything that occurs.

Keep them involved by inviting them to certain functions. It may well be that they will be glad of the arms-length nature of the agreement as it is one less property to manage, but they will also be grateful for the updates and will know you and your property should they ever need to take over its management.

A word of warning: what not to do

Sponsors keep a running record on properties within their portfolio and evaluate their performance regularly. I always had in place an evaluation system in which each property or event was graded against a set of variables which included the tangible and intangible benefits we had received. It rarely let me down.

The industry abounds with stories of ill-fated relationships that toppled under the failure of the sponsored organisation to honour or respect the terms of the agreement. An anecdote tells a thousand words and while the one that follows may seem pure fantasy, I'm afraid every word is true.

An edict came through from one of our senior executives that he had agreed to sponsor a major annual event. The fee was not chickenfeed; it was in the low six figures and could easily have satisfied the sponsorship needs of several worthy organisations. The administration and event management were passed on to me. As the organisation was a high-profile body with 'household name' status, I naively imagined that the task of management would be straightforward and painless: that the event would be managed with military precision. Mistake number one.

I expected, as would any reasonable sponsorship manager, that the organisation's personnel would be keen for dialogue and willing to bend over backwards to accommodate their new sponsor. After all, the event had been struggling for some time to attract sponsorship and was actually on the verge of collapse when we intervened. Mistake number two.

I had to chase these people for information and pry every promised benefit from them. I would have found shucking oysters bare-handed a far easier and more enjoyable task. It was plain hard work and focused precious resources on this one event, diverting time and effort from those problem-free properties and events that delivered everything as promised.

On one occasion the organisation called a meeting to discuss important aspects of their event. I arrived at the appointed place and time and sat in splendid isolation for some while before being informed that the organisation's two representatives had forgotten about the meeting and would not be able to make it. Is this a case of rudeness, or just plain stupidity? The jury is still out on that one!

The most soul-destroying aspect of the deal was that the contract was to run for three years. I knew I could look forward to the same problems and suffer the same headaches for the next two years. The organisation at no time actually breached the letter of the agreement but they sailed dangerously close to the wind on many occasions. Hardly the stuff of which renewed contracts are made.

Not surprisingly, the organisation was cut adrift as soon as the contract finished. In my opinion, the massive fees and the large amount of energy expended on this one organisation were tragically wasted. Amazingly the event limped and lurched around for the next few years. Tragically, despite a fine and proud history, it finally sank into oblivion. It was a great property, but tradition and pride can never carry an event like a professional and dedicated team that has have the passion and strength to push into the future.

An important lesson: never make the sponsor chase you.

No sponsor ever enters into an agreement expecting the onus of maintaining the relationship to rest solely with them. No busy sponsorship manager will willingly shoulder the burden of unnecessary workload. And remember, word travels fast in the industry.

We are all but mere mortals

A last word about your relationship with the representatives of your sponsor: in all your transactions, remember that you are dealing with people with feelings, not simply ever-fruiting money trees. Be genuine in your interest in them and you may well find that real friendships follow. When speaking to them, expand the conversation to include social chat and interaction. When all conversations revolve around the business side of sponsorship, the underlying text seems to read, 'gimme, gimme, gimme'.

And forget the adage, 'You can't keep all of the people happy all of the time'. Why not? Plan well, consider everyone's position, act with integrity and you have a good chance of keeping everybody happy. Yes, I know that sometimes an unpredictable fly alights in your ointment and things can become messy, but if you have a sound conflict-resolution strategy in place and remain true to your principles, the ointment can be returned to its pristine pre-fly condition without too much grief. And should things start to get too messy, remember the two golden rules:

Rule 1. The sponsor is always right.

Rule 2. When in doubt refer to Rule 1

FROM THE EXPERTS

What do you expect from your sponsorship partners in return for your support?

- ❖ 'I expect my partners to support me as I support them.'
- ❖ 'I want to have the ability to leverage [use] my involvement with events to benefit my company with the full support of the events I sponsor.'
- ❖ 'To abide by the original agreement, and not to keep coming up with "add-ons".' (Add-ons were explained as the sponsored organisation continually asking for more support

outside the contract conditions.)

❖ 'A strong working relationship that is mutually beneficial.'

LESSONS TO TAKE FROM THIS CHAPTER

❖ When you sign on the dotted line your work has just begun.
❖ Never, ever make the sponsor chase you.
❖ Obtain publicity for your event and your sponsor at every opportunity.
❖ Use your imagination – conjure up an idea that will make your sponsor feel special and therefore appreciated.
❖ Don't rely on your friendship with the CEO, managing director, or senior personnel – get to know their people.
❖ Keep all of your sponsors happy all of the time.

SUGGESTED RESEARCH EXERCISE

What does your organisation have that could be turned into an event or experience for your sponsor? Think outside the square and, initially at least, outside your budget. If you had unlimited resources, what would you do to stroke your sponsor's ego? Can you adjust this a little so that it falls within reach of your resources?

FURTHER READINGS

http://ambler.com/newwordpress/article-library/attracting-and-retaining-long-term-repeat-corporate-sponsors/

http://smartmeetings.com/event-planning-magazine/2010/02/10-ways-to-obtain-and-retain-sponsors

SPONSORSHIP FACT

During 2012, Education and Youth ranked 1st globally, with 44% of actual partnerships within Corporate Social Responsibility related segments.

Fourteen

Utilising the media

'All publicity is good, except for an obituary notice.'
BRENDAN BEHAN

At one stage, my company arranged to conduct a joint sales promotion with a leading newspaper. Readers were asked to send in a coupon from the paper for a chance to win a year's supply of packaged beer. A photo of a stack of beer was of no interest to the newspaper, so I enlisted the assistance of the late and great Jim Stynes, the Australian Rules football champion who was at the time well on his way to breaking the AFL record for the number of consecutive games played (which he did and still holds today). Jim, who was sponsored by my company at the time, was photographed sitting on top of the cartons of beer. The photo and article appeared on page two of the paper.

The promotion was a resounding success and offers an example of the enormous asset a sponsored party can be to its sponsors. Jim provided the 'big name' angle and the sponsor achieved its objectives. It was no great inconvenience or effort for Jim to arrive, sit on a few cartons and smile, and in fact he was delighted to do something for his sponsor. Be like Jim and willingly cooperate with your sponsors when they ask, but even more so, find your own opportunities to promote them whenever you can.

To ensure maximum effort towards gaining media interest, one person should be nominated to plan and coordinate media liaison within your organisation. Depending on your size, this may involve operating at local, regional, state and/or national level. Again, the appointee should possess all the traits we identified in Chapter Seven as essential in a sponsorship coordinator: a never-say-die attitude, a passion for your organisation and a tendency not to fall down in the presence of kryptonite.

Getting friendly with a journalist (or two, or three)

The job involves building a good relationship with journalists, which will not happen unless your media liaison person is reliable and cooperative. They can expect calls from reporters at odd times, such as – as often happened to me – very late or unbelievably early as they prepare copy for the next edition of their newspaper or magazine. When contacted, your representative should remain cooperative regardless of the inconvenience and either give the requested information fully or direct the journalist to a person who can. Here is my advice for your media liaison person:

- ❖ When dealing with the media, always be honest and direct. Help journalists do their job and they will look favourably on you and your organisation.
- ❖ If you don't know something, say so; don't guess or give a half-truth. Journalists will return to a source that is available, helpful, informed and provides honest copy with good quotes. They are busy people who cannot afford the time to make multiple phone calls, or the embarrassment of going to press with incorrect information.
- ❖ There may be times when you are unable to answer a question because your organisational policy expressly forbids it. Politely decline, explaining the situation and assuring the journalist that if the information should become available you will ring them. They will respect this stance, whereas a terse 'no comment' will not win a warm spot in the hearts of journos committed to a good story and driven by an impossible deadline.

The media you contact will depend on your organisation and its newsworthiness. A well-known charity, for example, might command the attention of the national press. A local horticultural society might be pressed to get much interest from the local newspaper, but if the story is interesting to others in the field it may get a run in a horticultural magazine. Make a list of your events and work out where best to target them, as in Figure 14.1.

A good publicity opportunity can shoot the lowest-profile group to prominence. It's up to your media liaison person to ensure that the best-possible level of media coverage is given to your organisation. Know your target: familiarise yourself with all areas of media. Read papers – local weeklies and dailies; listen to radio, watch television. Get a feel for the content and style of their stories, their writers and presenters: note where organisations such as yours are featured. Once you have an understanding of the options, arrange an appointment with key people: newspaper sub-editors or journalists, and television and radio producers. Give them a presentation about your organisation. This is best done when you have something of interest to offer them – perhaps a good story in the form of a press release.

Don't go to them only when you have a fundraiser coming up. If this is the only contact you make they will think you only want free publicity.

Figure 14.1: Event/media planner (charity organisations).

WHO	MAJOR HAPPENING	NEWS-WORTHY?	WHICH MEDIA?
War Veterans' Association	Local door knock	Minor	Community radio
Local Scouts	Car wash fundraiser	Minor	Local press
Anti Cancer Council	Sales of sunscreen and hats in regional centre	Medium	Regional commercial Radio & local press
Oxfam (UK)	Guinness Book of Records Attempt	Medium	State TV and newspapers
Red Cross	National annual sale of pins	High	National TV news National radio National newspapers

Most media need paid advertisements to survive: they are unlikely to offer you publicity for nothing. So don't be afraid to advertise your events and activities in the media with which you want to build a relationship. You will find that such a strategy pays dividends.

When writing a media release, always consider the section of the paper or magazine that it is aimed at. Find out who the relevant sub-editor is and send your media release directly to them, never to 'The Editor', who is not involved at this level. If you have built a good relationship with a journalist, contact them and tell them about the story, or fax your media release to both this journalist and the relevant sub-editor, letting each know that the other has a copy.

Finding an angle

You have about eight seconds to win a sub-editor's attention before they 'spike' the story and consign it to the 'nice story, but . . .' pile. Why eight seconds? A sub-editor I know once told me that he was under such continual pressure from print deadlines that eight seconds was the maximum time allowable to filter the vast quantity of newsworthy items that daily crossed his desk. Many of the articles were variations on recurring themes and he had to ensure he found items that had a 'fresh' approach and that fitted the style and tone of his newspaper.

Thus there are ways to pique the interest of a tired sub-editor who has seen it all before. Always try to put an angle on every media release story. So many similar stories cross a sub-editor's desk – yours should have an angle that sets it apart:

❖ Is there a big name connected to the story?
❖ A large amount of money?
❖ A broken national or world record?
❖ An unusual human-interest element?
❖ Is there some special significance attached to the event – an anniversary, a centenary?
❖ Is the location unusual?

When thinking about announcements or events, consider that the media will need to be lured by something special about the story.

Do not imagine that your story is so unique and fascinating that it will stop a newsroom dead with its charm or newsworthiness. Journalists are bombarded daily with promotional copy from organisations such as yours, so look for ways to make your material demand attention. Consider these scenarios:

❖ Your basketball club is having a family day. That's nice, but the only real value this has for a paper is as a free or paid advertisement in the community notices or classifieds.
❖ Your basketball club is having a family day to celebrate twenty-five years as a club and all past players are invited. This may get a run as a filler in a local paper.
❖ Your basketball club is having a family day and its founder, Joe Smith, who coincidentally turns 90 on the same day, will be there to draw the raffle. Will possibly attract a local paper to run an

article which will come from the angle of the birthday but cannot help mentioning your club.

❖ Your basketball club is having a family day and founder Joe Smith, who coincidentally turns 100 on the same day, will be trying to break the world record for the number of baskets shot by a centenarian. Will certainly attract local and probably daily paper and electronic media attention as a human-interest piece.

❖ Your basketball club is having a family day and US superstar LeBron James from the Miami Heat has agreed to fly in for the day and act as Mr. Smith's coach and trainer. Almost guaranteed national (and possibly international) news media attention.

Are you getting the idea? In the absence of an ancient but spritely founder with a sure aim and powerful contacts, you must look around for something that will generate media interest.

Writing a media release

Prepare your media release in a professional manner so that it can be converted into a story with as little work as possible. A media release is not a letter, nor is it a document that might open with the words: 'I thought you might be interested in . . .' It is a professionally prepared document of the type that newspaper people are used to dealing with. It should be no more than two pages in length and should be double-spaced with wide margins. See Figure 14.2 for an example. The information should be:

❖ about a genuinely newsworthy event
❖ factual and concise devoid of cliché
❖ written simply in plain, jargon-free English
❖ written in the active voice
❖ without repetition
❖ proofread for errors.

In addition, it should contain original, strong quotes and the names and numbers of people who can be contacted for further information. See the 'showbag of samples' at the back of this book for a further example of a media release.

When you are dealing with newspapers, offer to supply them with good-quality photos or give them a photo opportunity. Wherever possible, include your sponsor's logo in photos – on clothing or in the background. Use a pre printed backdrop that depicted your sponsorship hierarchy, or find a location that prominently features you sponsors. Journos will be happy to accommodate this in their pursuit of a good story. They understand sponsorship. They are accommodating and they play the game well.

Five Ws and an H

The media release should answer the six basic questions that readers want answered in any story: who, what, where, when, why and how. Journalists usually strive to answer the first two of these in the first sentence of a piece. Who did or will do what, to or for whom? Sometimes the place or the reason may be more important, in which case those elements will take pride of place. Remember, names are news and everyone is interested in large sums of money, so if you have a famous person involved or a financially large sponsorship deal to announce, put them right up there in the first few words. Grab the sub-editor's attention with the first sentence and your chances of inclusion increase considerably. If you present your media release in a bright, intelligently written way, it may be used in its entirety. Note that when removing material from an item to fit it into a smaller space in their publication, a sub-editor will usually cut from the bottom, so place your information in strict order of importance. Don't place a zinger in the tail – it may not be printed.

Figure 14.2 The anatomy of a media release

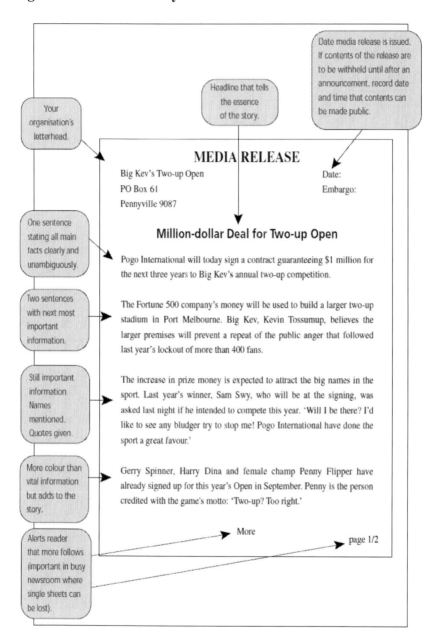

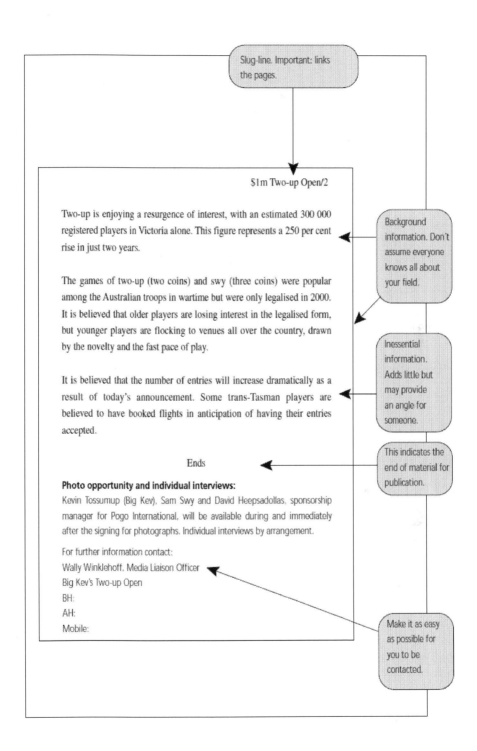

Slug-line. Important: links the pages.

$1m Two-up Open/2

Two-up is enjoying a resurgence of interest, with an estimated 300 000 registered players in Victoria alone. This figure represents a 250 per cent rise in just two years.

The games of two-up (two coins) and swy (three coins) were popular among the Australian troops in wartime but were only legalised in 2000. It is believed that older players are losing interest in the legalised form, but younger players are flocking to venues all over the country, drawn by the novelty and the fast pace of play.

It is believed that the number of entries will increase dramatically as a result of today's announcement. Some trans-Tasman players are believed to have booked flights in anticipation of having their entries accepted.

Ends

Photo opportunity and individual interviews:
Kevin Tossumup (Big Kev), Sam Swy and David Heepsadollas, sponsorship manager for Pogo International, will be available during and immediately after the signing for photographs. Individual interviews by arrangement.

For further information contact:
Wally Winklehoff, Media Liaison Officer
Big Kev's Two-up Open
BH:
AH:
Mobile:

Background information. Don't assume everyone knows all about your field.

Inessential information. Adds little but may provide an angle for someone.

This indicates the end of material for publication.

Make it as easy as possible for you to be contacted.

Using a public relations consultant

Press releases are a valuable tool, so if you feel you cannot do them justice you may want to consider giving the job to a public relations firm. This is especially advisable if the information to be disseminated is controversial. Suppose a member of your organisation was involved in a nasty fist fight outside a bar and was photographed wearing clothing featuring your sponsor's logo. The services of an experienced public relations consultant could be invaluable in structuring an approach to neutralise the adverse situation and to assist in placating the sponsor.

Whether or not this is an option for your organisation will depend on the health of its bank account, but no matter how easily the cost fits into your budget, monitor the effectiveness of the service. Are you getting value for money? Are you getting the media coverage you want – both in quantity and quality? To give your public relations consultant the best chance, prepare a very detailed brief from which they can work.

Ensuring coverage for your sponsors

High on the guest list of any event should be your media contacts. Your media liaison officer should be designated the task of ensuring that these people have received their invitations and are coming. Another critical task is that of ensuring that the media people meet the sponsors. Ideally, place the sponsors and Media representatives close together when arranging the seating. This allows for a more extended conversation and may result in greater coverage for the sponsors. Even if such coverage is not forthcoming, the sponsor will see that you are actively working to their benefit – that you are managing your event in order to achieve the best results for them.

I can think of many newsworthy events I attended where the organisers had not even thought to invite the media, and another opportunity went begging. Don't be a media mug. Invite them to anything you believe is worthy of coverage, but be aware of the difference between what excites your organisation and what will excite a more diverse readership or audience. Select your events very carefully and your media contacts will know that you can be relied on to provide them with real news opportunities.

For example, cable television has been a bonus to all sports and in particular the horse racing industry. The racing clubs were quick to see the potential to boost the interests of sponsors. I have lost count of the number of times I was interviewed on cable television or the number of times my presentation speech to a winner was broadcast to thousands of bars and clubs across the nation. I was interviewed on local and community radio stations, did countless interviews for newspapers and magazines and was featured on local, regional and interstate television. None of this media exposure was initiated by me; the overwhelming majority was arranged by organisations that I had sponsored. They had it right.

Each communication medium (television, radio, newspapers and so on) is a tool of survival. If you have not yet involved them in your organisation, act now.

LESSONS TO TAKE FROM THIS CHAPTER

- ❖ The media can be your friends, but you must approach them in a professional manner.
- ❖ You have a greater chance of publicity if you have an angle to your stories.
- ❖ A media release will be more appealing to a busy journalist or sub-editor if it is prepared in a professional manner and follows an accepted format.
- ❖ Always invite the media to your newsworthy events.

SUGGESTED RESEARCH EXERCISES

1. Do you know a journalist? If not, can you arrange an introduction to one? Ask if you can interview them for twenty or thirty minutes. Briefly describe your organisation. Ask what sort of things organisations such as yours might do to attract interest from the media. What sorts of angles are preferred?

2. Look through that pile of newspapers I asked you to examine in the exercise in Chapter One. Search for the sort of articles that might have been generated by a media release. How well do they read? Do they appear to convey the organisation's meaning and intention? Now work backwards: write a media release using such an article and the example of a media release given in the 'showbag of samples' at the end of this book.

3. Find a story in your organisation that could be the basis of an article and think of a clever angle that would be likely to grab a journalist's interest. Write the media release.

1. SPONSORSHIP PRESS RELEASE EXAMPLE

John Deere Announces Sponsorship of PGA TOUR Player Zach Johnson

2014 News Releases and Information

MOLINE, Illinois (February 18, 2014) – John Deere today announced it has become a corporate sponsor for professional golfer Zach Johnson, the seventh-ranked player in the Official World Golf Rankings. The arrangement further strengthens Deere's commitment to golf by building on its role as a title sponsor of a PGA TOUR event and as the TOUR's official supplier of golf course equipment.

Beginning with this week's World Golf Championship event in Marana, AZ, the well-known John Deere trademark will be displayed on Johnson's golf bag at all events he plays during the tenure of the multi-year sponsorship deal.

Johnson has won 11 PGA TOUR events including the 2007 Masters. He has also played on three Ryder Cup and three Presidents Cup teams.

"We admire Zach Johnson as a competitor and for the overall values he exemplifies in his life," said James Field, president of Deere's Worldwide Agriculture & Turf Division. "We believe Zach represents the core values for which the John Deere brand is known. He has unquestioned integrity, has displayed great commitment to his profession, family and community, and is one of the highest quality players in the game today."

Field said while the sponsorship has definite business objectives of promoting the John Deere brand name, it also is important to note that a portion of the company's sponsorship goes to the Zach Johnson Foundation, which focuses on children and families in need.

Johnson's relationship with Deere's professional golf tournament is longstanding. He received sponsor exemptions to play in the John Deere Classic both in 2002 and 2003 before he earned a full-time PGA TOUR membership. He won the John Deere Classic in 2012, has been runner-up twice, and has played in the tournament 12 straight years. Johnson also is a member of the tournament's executive committee.

"It is a privilege to represent John Deere, one of the world's most admired companies," said Johnson. "It is a significant responsibility to be entrusted with representing a company known around the world for its strong values. I am sincerely looking forward to it."

About John Deere

Deere & Company (NYSE: DE) is a world leader in providing advanced products and services and is committed to the success of customers whose work is linked to the land - those who cultivate, harvest, transform, enrich and build upon the land to meet the world's dramatically increasing need for food, fuel, shelter and infrastructure. Since 1837, John Deere has delivered innovative products of superior quality built on a tradition of integrity. For more information, visit John Deere at its worldwide website at www.JohnDeere.com.

For further information, the news media should call:

Ken Golden
Director, Global Public Relations
Deere & Company

309-765-5678

2. SPONSORSHIP PRESS RELEASE EXAMPLE

Ditto Music Launches Chartbreaker Promo Bundle

Online Music Publishing Service Launches New Service Designed to Get Independent Artists to the Top of the Charts

FOR IMMEDIATE RELEASE

*PRLog (Press Release) - **Feb. 28, 2014 - LONDON, U.K.** -- Online Music Publishing Service Launches New Service Designed to Get Independent Artists to the Top of the Charts*

Music distribution specialist Ditto Music has announced the launch of its Chartbreaker package (http://www.dittomusic.com/lp/chartbreaker/), which has been designed to give aspiring independent recording artists everything they need to reach the top of the charts.

The limited-edition bundle - usually worth over £440 - is being made available for just £89, and it includes two of Ditto's latest music publishing innovations - the iTunes Pre-Release Service and a revolutionary SMS ordering service.

Independent artists who purchase the Chartbreaker Bundle will also be able to create their very own iTunes profile page, which allows them to create a distinctive identity whilst improving the buying experience for fans.

And perhaps most important of all, Ditto's huge network of contacts and relationships in the music industry means artists can also sell their work via more than 200 online music stores and streaming sites, including iTunes, Spotify, Bloom FM and Google Play.

With options to register material in all of the world's major music charts, including the Official UK Chart and all the Billboard Charts, independent artists have a fantastic opportunity to further the reach of their material and forge a career in a notoriously tough industry. For people with talent and the necessary determination to succeed in the cutthroat business of music, the Chartbreaker Bundle can make their dreams of fame and fortune come true.

"The Chartbreaker Bundle (http://www.dittomusic.com/lp/chartbreaker/) is about putting the power back into the recording artist's hands. We believe that talented people should be allowed the freedom to shape their own career, and the innovative services included in this package should help them to do that."

Another significant advantage to signing up for Ditto's Chartbreaker Bundle is that artists get to keep all their royalties through the setting up of their own record label.

The Chartbreaker Bundle's iTunes Pre-Release service also gives fans the opportunity to download free sample tracks when they pre-order an independent artist's album or EP. This new feature from Ditto will allow artists to build a following and create an element of hype around an upcoming release.

The new SMS feature included in the package allows consumers to pre-order music directly from their mobile device - giving loyal fans the heads-up about upcoming single and album releases.

"There are thousands of highly gifted and motivated recording artists throughout Europe who simply can't catch a break when it comes to getting a recording contract. However, by making their music available to fans in a range of ways, providing fans with exclusive preview material and building the hype around a new release, artists now have the chance to emulate the world's biggest music stars.'

About Ditto Music

Ditto Music (http://www.dittomusic.com/) is a publishing specialist dedicated to giving independent recording artists a chance at becoming published artists. Ditto allows all its artists to keep 100% of their royalties. And through a range of innovative music distribution services and marketing opportunities, Ditto is committed to helping independent recording artists to realise their dreams.

Contact Ditto Music

All press enquiries should be made by emailing Ditto Music at lee@dittomusic.com or by telephoning on 0151 9093577.

Registered address:
Ditto Music UK
31 Parliament Street
Liverpool L8 5RN

Contact
Lee Parsons
0151 9093577
***@dittomusic.com

PRESS RELEASE QUESTIONS
- JOHN DEERE AND DITTO MUSIC

1. You have read and digested the rationale behind the anatomy of a press release in Figure 14.2. Can you now identify in both the John Deere and Ditto Music press releases, all of the:
    ❖ Who, what, where, and?
    ❖ When, why, how?

  And also can you detect the:
    ❖ who did what/will do what?
    ❖ and who did/will do what for whom?

Now, take some paper and a pen and draw up a table with all of the above points and fill in the gaps from the John Deere release and the Ditto release. Do that with as many press releases as you can find and have time for. You will get the hang of it fairly quickly and this exercise will hone your skills at press release writing. When the time comes, you will be in a great position to craft and disseminate an attractive, informative and complete press release.

SPONSORSHIP FACT

Anheuser-Busch has been the top spender in the last five Super Bowls, investing $149 million between the years, 2009-2013. That places the brewer of Budweiser and Bud Light as the foremost supporter of the NFL championship.

Fifteen

Maintaining your sponsorships

'You can have everything in life you want, if you will
just help enough people get what they want.'
ZIG ZIGLAR

So you have a group of sponsors who are happily supporting your organisation. Congratulations – they are a fine-looking bunch and probably the result of much hard work on your part. But don't rest on your laurels and allow your control of the situation to slip. Your role may change at this point, but it is important that you maintain and oversee your relationships, watching and planning for problems long before they occur.

You have an ethical responsibility to ensure that your sponsors feel they belong. There are sound commercial reasons for your continued attention, so live by the credo, 'The sponsor is royalty.' Sponsors rule because it is through their contributions that your organisation survives in this cut-throat competitive world. Treat them well and they will tell others. Treat them poorly and they will also tell others, and very quickly. Of course, this will reduce your future opportunities.

Usually your benefactor group consists of one major sponsor and a number of other companies or individuals whose financial contributions are smaller. Consider your entire group of sponsors and question the balance.

What if . . . ?

What if your major sponsor gave notice of their company's intention to withdraw support from your organisation? Or what if a sponsor providing a lower level of support dropped out?

I'm sure you will immediately grasp the significance of the first hypothetical loss. There can be no doubt that the sudden withdrawal of such support would cause immense difficulty. I'm also sure that you would assess the minor loss as a mere ripple, having far less impact; after all, a minor sponsor will be far easier to replace.

I remember a phone call from a frantic committee member of a prominent country horse-racing club. His major sponsor had informed him that his company would not be renewing its contract. He told me that his club's annual cup-day meeting was fast approaching and he did not have a naming rights sponsor for the premier event on that day. Despite his best efforts, he had not been able to persuade anyone to finance the race at such short notice. In desperation, and to ensure a high-profile corporate identity was associated with the club's main (and nationally advertised) event, he offered naming rights to the event to my company for 10 per cent of the fee paid by the original sponsor. I accepted his offer and my company reaped all of the benefits from the naming rights for a minimal payment – in fact, the price we paid should have secured only a minor support sponsor role. By not identifying and nurturing a replacement major sponsor, the racing club missed out on a large slice of funding to support its major annual event.

Though this may seem a bizarre situation, it was far from an isolated case. I have observed the phenomenon many times:
- ❖ sometimes it's complacency ('This relationship is sacrosanct and eternal');
- ❖ sometimes it is a refusal to face the possibility of separation ('If I don't think about it, it won't happen').

Whatever the reason, the sponsored organisation believed that it was joined at the hip to its sponsor and failed to plan for the loss. In such a case, when the amputation occurs, the haemorrhage is severe.

Anticipating change

Plan for all the 'what ifs' that might come your way. Organisations lose sponsors. The circumstances that led to your partnership three years ago might well have altered beyond recognition. They may no longer need the association with you to achieve their goals; their profits might have plummeted and they're pulling back from sponsorship for the duration of their difficulties. They might withdraw part of their funding or pack up and move out completely. Life is like that. So start planning for all contingencies.

Of course there are exceptions to the rule, as in the case of the AFL club Geelong and the Ford Motor Company. Graeme Johnstone, Geelong's affable former marketing manager, tells me that the car manufacturer has sponsored the club continuously since 1925! That phenomenal partnership must be the envy of all sponsored organisations. I suspect that it is probably the most enduring relationship of its kind in Australia and possibly the world (certainly up there with Coca Cola's continuing sponsorship of the Olympic Games). It has been a most impressive achievement that must indicate a precise matching of needs and goals.

However, Ford has recently announced a shut down of all manufacturing in Australia during October 2016 due to rising costs and a decline in sales. The company stated that it had incurred losses over the past five years (to end of June 2013) of more than $600 million. So, Ford is bleeding money and is suffering from a loss in sales. Not a healthy climate in which to pump a reputed $1 million per annum into the club, therefore what of the sponsorship deal? What is the board of the Ford Motor Company thinking about the current and future arrangement? What is the board of Geelong Football Club contemplating about its deal with Ford? Although Geelong has put on a brave face publicly stating that they believe the arrangement will endure, no concrete information is forthcoming. Thus by pure speculation, I feel that the AFL club may have tucked away a contingency plan for scouting for a replacement naming rights sponsor.

In addition, as at February 2014, The Football Association (FA) headquartered in the United Kingdom has yet to secure a new major naming rights sponsor for the FA Cup. The major sponsor Budweiser decided not to renew its £9 million a year deal for the 2014-15 competition. The fee is only a small portion of the overall income (estimated a total of £318m last season), derived from the competition.

However, the FA had a £228 million net debt at 31 December 2012 incurred from the massive cost of building Wembley Stadium. In addition the FA paid £25 million in net interest and finance costs. So in terms of the £9 million loss in major sponsorship, every penny counts. Therefore the FA has acknowledged that sponsorship is a key elements of it's financial health.

Where did things go wrong? Nothing sinister, a simple business resolution for a change in direction and strategy. The decision not to renew the agreement was pre-empted by a change of personnel and objectives at the US parent company Anheuser-Busch. The company has resolved to focus on the forthcoming FIFA World Cup in Brazil and has committed to the 2018 and 2022 tournaments. In addition Budweiser will allocate sponsorship funding to music projects.

On a brighter note though, it has been reported that the FA is in the USA to discuss details with four possible main sponsors, hoping to agree to a deal a little above the £32m over four years which was paid by Budweiser.

The FA is hoping that the next sponsor will not be a bookmaker, beer or high-calorie food brand, which are saturating sports sponsorships. The organisation is optimistic that it will secure a solid replacement sponsorship for its competition.

Further, in 2012 the mobile services company Orange, which had at that time joined with T-Mobile to form the UK's largest communications company, withdrew its support of the prestigious "prize for women's fiction" in order to focus on film industry sponsorship. The prize for had borne the Orange name since the award's inception in 1995. At that time, it was the longest continuous arts sponsorship in the UK, Even so, the Orange pronouncement was a commercial one where the company made a conscious decision to focus on film industry sponsorship. This and the previous example demonstrate that there is no sentiment in the sponsorship arena.

After about twelve months after the Orange withdrawal, Bailey's liquor was announced as the new sponsor.

Like the examples above, if your organisation finds itself faced with the sudden loss of an important sponsor and no backup plan in place, then I'm afraid that there is only one answer: start again. But this time there is probably more pressure, because you, like the racing club, might have to work to an impossible time frame. This will invariably lead to desperate moves, including concession of additional benefits and a greatly reduced fee, all of which are detrimental to your goals and damaging to your organisation's image. To use the 'hills and valleys' model (discussed in an earlier chapter), you are in such a deep valley that the hilltop will be almost out of earshot when you make your plea.

With forward planning, this situation need never arise, and if the feared sponsorship withdrawal does happen, it will cause only a minor headache.

Figure 15.1 The sudden loss of a sponsor dilemma

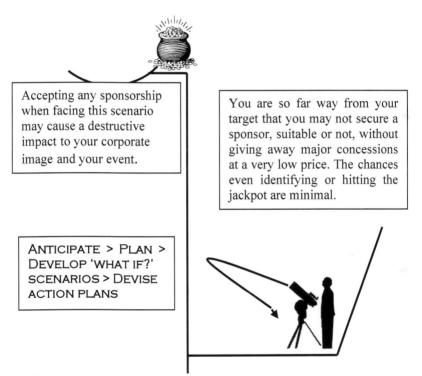

Accepting any sponsorship when facing this scenario may cause a destructive impact to your corporate image and your event.

You are so far way from your target that you may not secure a sponsor, suitable or not, without giving away major concessions at a very low price. The chances even identifying or hitting the jackpot are minimal.

ANTICIPATE > PLAN > DEVELOP 'WHAT IF?' SCENARIOS > DEVISE ACTION PLANS

The hierarchy of sponsors

Having acknowledged the indisputable truth that you cannot keep a sponsor forever, start planning for a possible future without them. Draw up a hierarchy of your sponsors, placing those giving the most support on top and moving down to those making the least contribution (see Figure 15.2). Break these down into categories, assigning a level label to them. For example, you might choose to call the uppermost the gold level, followed by silver, then bronze. Or major and minor, or A, B and C. The choice of name is not important, just the fact of categorisation, which helps to build a framework around your hierarchy.

You might already do this quite well, but to what purpose? Traditionally, the hierarchy has been used solely to divide sponsorship into segments denoting levels of support, and perhaps encourage lower-level sponsors to aspire to a higher level. My belief is that it can and should be used to embrace a third key concept: the identification and encouragement of new sponsors (see Figure 15.3).

Figure 15.2: Traditional hierarchy of sponsors

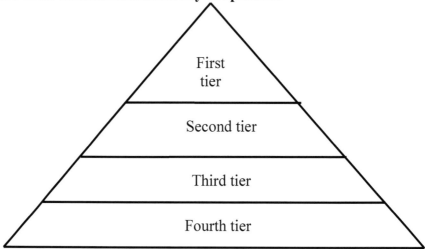

In the hierarchy above (figure 15.2), sponsors are simply ranked from those providing the lowest financial input to those providing the highest level of commitment.

The improved hierarchy (Figure 15.3) identifies and develops sponsors on lower levels who can replace or join sponsors on higher levels. Use each tier as a springboard for sponsors to advance up the hierarchy, and reposition sponsors who wish to reduce their level of support by finding a more suitable lower-level tier for them.

The tiers in the hierarchy

Let's examine the tiers in the hierarchy and look at what sponsors expect from their involvement. We will have to try a little amateur psychology to determine why sponsors would want to be placed on a certain tier.

Major sponsor

As we have already established, the major sponsor is probably supporting your organisation for strategic reasons. They are using a sponsorship strategy to acquire advantages for their organisation. These might include any one or more of the following:
- ❖ networking opportunities with members or other sponsors
- ❖ some tangible benefit from the association with your event or image (such as increased sales or sampling opportunities)
- ❖ enhancement of the organisation's standing as a good citizen
- ❖ increased consumer awareness
- ❖ use of the property for competitive advantage.

Figure 15.3: The improved hierarchy of sponsors.

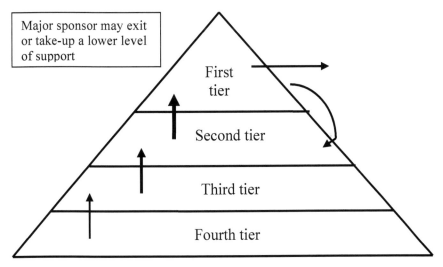

The position of major sponsor can also deliver very high exposure within the target market of the sponsored organisation and can present a perception of high involvement and a sense of ownership.

Then again, the sponsorship may simply be an act of charity or even an ego-driven decision. As discussed in Chapter Thirteen, owners, directors or senior executives will sponsor for a multitude of reasons when there is absolutely no commercial reason for doing so.

The major sponsor, then, is a firm or individual with the financial resources and motivation to be in that position. The fee payable for the privilege may preclude others from the major sponsorship role, so these others will take up a rank that matches the most they can afford.

For example, your lower-level sponsors may have similar desires and motivations to be your major sponsor, but resources disqualify them from the position. The only factor keeping them from this coveted position is their inability to pay the asking price. They will therefore take up a position in your hierarchy that they can afford. The major sponsor may also have simply out-bid the other sponsors if the sponsorship was too attractive to lose.

Joint major sponsors

At this point I would like to offer a word about taking on joint major sponsors. That word is, Don't. The sage warning against being at the service of two masters has never been as true as it is in the sponsorship field. Unless you can guarantee that you will be scrupulously even-handed in your distribution of benefits and exposure to each, you are flirting with disaster. Naturally you will start out with the right intentions and make every effort to see that both are given equal rights. Then sponsor X will generously throw in a few more dollars or offer some extra funding and pretty soon sponsor X is reaping the rewards of the increased support. That's fine, but sponsor Y, who came into the agreement anticipating equal rights under the existing financial arrangements, has every right to expect the same treatment. This sponsor will be extremely displeased that, to regain equality, they have to up the ante. When one of your 'joint' sponsors gains the upper hand, you will be left scrambling to redress the balance and facing a major conflict as each demands their rights – rights that you promised.

When I inherited joint arrangements I immediately took steps either to withdraw from the partnership or to pay the difference to gain sole position as major sponsor.

If you are having to consider joint major sponsors, ask yourself, Am I asking too much money? The answer is almost certainly yes. Given that you have presented your figures and explained your planned use of the money, if a major sponsor is unwilling to pay the full sponsorship fee asked then they have probably judged that your figures are too high or your operation is not offering them enough benefits. Either way your value in the market is not equal to your asking price.

Sponsorship managers do not like to fight with other sponsors over the same property and it is difficult to persuade all parties to agree equally on everything. Keep your sanity and if you find yourself considering taking on joint major sponsors, push the temptation firmly aside.

Second-tier sponsors

Some companies that are either unwilling or unable to pay a major sponsorship fee will prefer a spot on the second tier. This position allows them the freedom to be involved with an event or property without having to commit to such a large financial input. And if all their objectives from the relationship are met by this tier, then why not? Usually this level offers sponsors exclusive rights in their category. For example, an ice-cream manufacturer on the second tier will be the only ice-cream purveyor permitted to sponsor you and will be guaranteed sole rights for ice-cream sales at events. Under these terms, all the advertising and awareness benefits received from the property are outweighed by the lure of exclusive sales and locking their competitors out.

Somewhere on this second tier there will also usually be a different class of sponsor: a 'major sponsor in the wings'. This is the company that would have liked the position of major sponsor but was blocked by your existing arrangement. Don't let such potential slip through your fingers. Pamper and nurture them – they are your insurance, your safety net should the first tier suddenly become vacant. Then when the dreaded news that your major sponsor is withdrawing arrives, your way is easy and obvious. If you have cultivated a 'sponsor in the wings', you can answer that 'what if . . .' posed earlier in this chapter quite satisfactorily.

Another group of sponsors who may sit on this second tier neither covet the major sponsor position nor desire category exclusivity. They may be diehard supporters or be driven by some other desire to support a particular organisation, but have a limit on the fee they are willing to pay for the title of sponsor. Numbers on this tier can vary and will depend on the number of tangible benefits available for distribution between them.

Third-tier sponsors

Here you would expect to find a greater number of sponsors who will pay considerably less for the privilege of sponsorship and in return receive fewer benefits than those on the higher tiers. Small companies, firms and individuals usually fit into this level.

To many, this level is as high as they ever want to go. Given that these sponsors are usually far less wealthy than those above them, any financial commitment can be a costly experience. They look upon the support they give you as an investment that allows them the opportunity to network with larger organisations. The business links they forge through their sponsorship can be extremely valuable and many a new deal has been negotiated through a well-organised sponsor network.

Fourth-tier sponsors

The fourth tier may be the platform initially used to attract and win sponsors to your organisation. This level does not require a large financial commitment and allows a sponsor to test compatibility with your property. Your job is to ensure that this level of sponsor feels good about their involvement with your organisation and the idea of any further association with it. Such feelings might well result in a desire to climb up the hierarchy and achieve the recognition enjoyed at the higher levels.

This fourth tier is often populated by companies and individuals that supply goods in kind – meat trays, restaurant dinners or other of their products or services as raffle prizes, or holidays to auction. The benefits to you both are apparent. Your organisation derives revenue from the donation and the sponsor has their goods exposed to your members and their contacts.

Potential and target sponsors

In Figure 15.4 I have placed an extra level into the hierarchy that is not normally viewed as part of the sponsor set. This stratum holds the pool of potential sponsors from which you could draw new sponsors into your organisation. While theory might exclude this tier, I argue that it is the base on which you should build your hierarchy and through which you will ensure its continued viability. This is where you attend to potential sponsors with care and diligence.

The beauty is that on this level you have time on our side. Your seduction can be slow – no pressure, no hard sell. Your tools of seduction might include personal contact, inclusion in regular mail-outs and invitations to events and functions where these firms or individuals can rub shoulders with existing sponsors. Be patient and let the potential sponsors' own observations sell your property.

In figure 15.3, targets should be approached with a view to negotiating them into a predetermined level of the hierarchy based on your knowledge about them. Remember, you have time on your hands to pamper and encourage potential sponsors.

Figure 15.4: The improved hierarchy of sponsors (including potential and target sponsors).

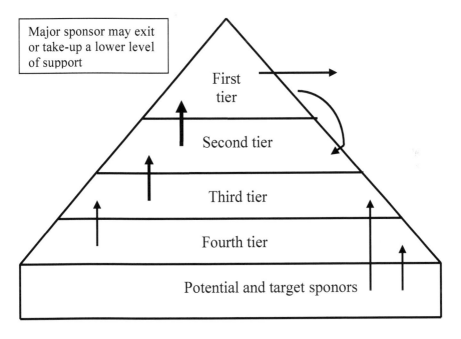

Recognition levels

Figure 15.5 suggests recognition levels for the various tiers of sponsor at a hypothetical event. Study it to get a feel for how you might best allocate all the benefits of your event so that sponsors receive what they have paid for. Once you list the benefits against the sponsor levels in this way, it becomes fairly straightforward to distinguish one level from another. By developing such a matrix, you can use it as a mechanism to guard against lower-level sponsors receiving benefits to which they are not entitled, or high-level sponsors missing out on their entitlements.

LESSONS TO TAKE FROM THIS CHAPTER

- ❖ Your organisation should have a hierarchical system that clearly denotes a sponsor's input.
- ❖ Be wary of appointing joint major sponsors.
- ❖ Watch for signs of willingness in lower-order sponsors to rise up the hierarchy.
- ❖ Underpin your hierarchy with potential target sponsors.

SUGGESTED RESEARCH EXERCISE

Look at your current list of sponsors.

- ❖ Which ones are clearly in for the long haul?
  - o Can you nominate any likely candidates for a higher position on the hierarchy?
  - o How many will pull out at the end of their commitment?
  - o Are any more likely to stay if they are offered a lower position with less financial outlay?
  - o Is there a potential major sponsor in the lower ranks?

FIGURE 15.5 HYPOTHETICAL RECOGNITION LEVELS

	PLATINUM	**GOLD**	**SILVER**	**BRONZE**
NAMING RIGHTS	Yes	No	No	No
ADVERTISING	All correspondence, press releases, comms & uniforms	Support and secondary to major	Spot adverts	No
TICKETING	All events x 20	All events x 10	All events x 4	All events x 2

SIGNAGE	Prominent - extensive and in prime television locations	Prominent: not to overshadow naming rights sponsor	Mixed with other silver sponsors	No
INIVTATIONS	All events & functions x 20	All x 4	All x 2	No
NEWSLETTERS	Major feature	Spot logos	Spot logo	No
MERCHANDISING	Logo on all merch items produced and sold at venues	In conjunction with other Gold	With other silver	No
POINT OF SALE MATERIAL	Extensive	Support to major	Selected events	Selected minor events
PROGRAM GUIDES	Logo on front cover and prominently featured throughout	Logo	Logo	Logo
PRODUCT CATEGORY EXCLUSIVITY	Yes	Yes	No	No
PROMOTIONAL OPPORTUNITIES	Yes	As agreed	Minimal	No
WEBSITE	Yes	Yes	Minimal	No
PRODUCT SAMPLING	Extensive	As agreed	Limited	No

Sixteen

Renegotiating your sponsorships

'Expecting something for nothing is the
most popular form of hope.'
ARNOLD GLASOW

So your sponsorship agreement is due for renewal. What are you going to do? I shall assume that you have not broken any of the sponsorship commandments listed in Chapter Thirteen, and that therefore you will renegotiate from a much stronger position. Your relative position has improved since you sat outside the sponsorship manager's office, perched on the edge of your seat, rehearsing all the wonderful things you would eventually forget to say. This time you will return to that chair and enter that office with a mutually satisfying relationship behind you. You might have been into the inner sanctum several times since the agreement was first signed and by now you will feel at ease. You know what to expect of the sponsor and they know what to expect of you.

When to renegotiate

The renegotiation process must, of necessity, be given time and thought. When you consider that at the peak of my company's sponsorship involvement I was administering some 2500 individual sponsorships, you will understand my reluctance – in fact, inability – to renegotiate them each year. Most sponsorship managers in my survey stated that they commenced renegotiations prior to the expiry of existing agreements.

The time frame varied a little, with many preferring to begin well in advance of the expiry date. Almost all of the managers said that they would instigate renegotiation. I believe this is probably due not so much to protocol but to the fact that these people are professionals whose job it is to keep everything running smoothly. Usually the person responsible for sponsorships at a club or organisation is working in a voluntary capacity and so does not have the time or experience to think about renewal until the contract has almost run its course.

The setting for the meeting

Providing your relationship with the sponsorship manager is good, the setting of the renegotiation meeting is somewhat less important than when you first came to present your credentials and proposal. Now you can safely take your negotiations outside the formal setting of an office. A cafe or restaurant is quite acceptable for renegotiation if you are comfortable with the other person and they are obviously at ease with you. Please be warned, though, that you should not lose sight of the reason you have come. Don't allow the more convivial surroundings to disguise the sobriety of the occasion. The partaking of alcohol or the ordering of food is best delayed until settlement is reached. Until then, allow nothing stronger than caffeine to drive your negotiations.

Negotiation skills – latent in us all

Are you a negotiator? The answer is an unequivocal -Yes. I can state that fairly confidently without having met you and without knowing anything about you. Why? Because you negotiate every day – at home, at work, with friends, at the shopping centre. Most human transactions involve some degree of give and take, and that is the essence of negotiation. Take a fairly average weekend in a typical family home:

Dad: 'Will you please mow the front lawn today?'

Son: 'Yes I will dad, but I need $20.'

Dad: 'OK, I will give you $20, but for that I want you to cut the front lawn and clean up the garage.'

Son: 'No way dad. I'll do both jobs for $30 – but I can't do either of them until tomorrow.'

Dad: 'No deal son, I need the front lawn mowed today so I'll give you $10 if you do by 3pm. It's now 2pm so you have better get a move on.'

Son: 'But I need $20 now dad to go to the movies and get a hamburger. So, how about I do the front lawn today and I clean up the backyard tomorrow…but you give me the $20 today?'

Dad: 'You drive a hard bargain son, but it's a deal.'

In this instance, everyone is happy. Many negotiations do not result in such bilateral victory – that win–win we are aiming for in sponsorship – but both parties will be trying to secure the best deal for themselves.

Figure 18.1 shows the possible outcomes of a negotiation.

Figure 18.1 : Negotiation outcomes.

WIN — WIN	Both parties are satisfied with the negotiations and they have received the benefits they sought in return for acceptable promises. Here you have what may be the start of an excellent working relationship.
WIN — LOSE	One party has received the benefits sought through the negotiating process. The other has either had to concede or has lost out on benefits that they expected in return for what they promised. Here you have a 'lopsided' relationship, one not conducive to a good working relationship.
LOSE— LOSE	Both parties have lost out and might have had to concede major points during the negotiation. In this scenario, neither party will be satisfied with the outcome and there may be difficulty in the two parties working successfully together. In the sponsorship arena such a result could be a recipe for disaster.

Recognise and rectify any weaknesses

You may feel confident about personal negotiations but less so when it comes to negotiating on behalf of your organisation. Skill and confidence grow only from experience, so please allow yourself every opportunity to learn through exposure to situations that require negotiation. Take note of the ways you deal with Certain circumstances and the effectiveness of your strategies. Review your performance afterwards and see where your weaknesses lie. If a pattern emerges that demonstrates an area where you need improvement, work on it.

I renegotiated several times over a period of years with a representative from a sporting organisation. Each time, this fellow was prepared to allow unnecessary major concessions in order to seal an agreement. His recurring error was in not seeking something in return for the additional benefits foregone. An experienced sponsorship manager will immediately realise that this type of negotiation cannot result in a win–win outcome and therefore the arrangement could become unworkable. Here the sponsorship seeker should have been provided with training and made aware that negotiations need to satisfy both parties to be deemed successful.

The majority of people you will face across the negotiation table will be old hands at this business. Give yourself the best chance of meeting them as equals.

Preparation is still vital

If your sponsor has no reason to withdraw support from your organisation, they will probably invite you to renegotiate your deal for a further term and you may regard yourself as more than halfway to the re-signing. If both parties are happy with the arrangement your negotiation should be fairly simple and hassle-free. But don't naively imagine that re-signing is a mere formality – you still have to work to secure the deal.

Prepare as much supporting information as you can to demonstrate how well you performed for the sponsor during the course of the expiring contract. This is the evidence that shows you kept all aspects of the agreement. Don't forget to mention all the little extras you threw in out of the sheer good-heartedness and warm-spiritedness of your organisation.

Again your aim is a win–win outcome, so be diligent in your preparation. Develop a presentation that gives all actual and estimated costings. This time you can be much closer to the mark because you are working from experience.

You should determine what you can and can't give, and what you must have, would like to have and really don't need. You should also assess fairly accurately what the sponsor wants from the deal and the order in which they might prioritise their needs. Include all the adjustments that had to be made during the sponsorship. Delete all those benefits the sponsor did not seem to need or use. Add all those benefits that the sponsor desires and that you are able to offer. To add interest to your offering, and to make the package more desirable, prepare a set of alternatives so that the sponsor has a series of options to consider. This is your opportunity to 'sell up' or promote your sponsor to a higher tier in the hierarchy.

Strategic manoeuvres

Don't assume that you know exactly what your sponsor wants. Their thinking might have shifted somewhat since your last round of talks. Listen carefully and employ the same basic strategies of negotiation that you used at the first face-to-face meeting (see Chapter Eleven). No, you don't have to begin at the beginning. At the meetings when your sponsor first became involved, you started to build your relationship and it has developed nicely during the period of the contract. But some of the advice I gave about the first meeting applies to all subsequent ones, and most importantly at renegotiation time.

Keep your renegotiation strategy simple and, above all, flexible. Only speak when you have something to say and allow your sponsor to finish talking before making your response. Renegotiation is not a time for 'relaxed and chatty' intercourse. Keep negotiations on track and don't be drawn into irrelevant topics or arguments where you lose control. The other party will then be controlling the content and direction of the meeting and you will find it extremely hard to get back in control. Don't be tempted into flippancy. Certainly humour is acceptable when appropriate, but never allow overconfidence to turn you into the 'clown prince'. This is important stuff – be serious about it. The time for play is after everything has been signed and sealed.

Sometimes a wily sponsorship manager will try to panic you into a quick resolution by citing a deadline by which everything must be finalised. Don't be fooled. Most timelines are negotiable.

If negotiations come to a standstill, don't panic. Remember that you have constraints governing what you can offer and so does your sponsor. A stalemate over one point doesn't mean that the entire process must be abandoned. The fact that you are both negotiating implies that you both hope to gain something of value from the successful completion of the negotiations. Be prepared to make concessions, but make sure that for each one you give, you receive one in return. Think of each concession given without a balancing one in your favour as a loss to you.

Non-verbal signals

Look for the signals – eyes and body cues indicate how things are proceeding, but although they are good signs, they should not be relied on solely. What tone of voice is your sponsor using and does it rise or fall, quicken or slow at important points in the negotiation?

A while back I attended a meeting with Alan Dymond of Bridge Marketing Group, a firm of marketing consultants with which I had a consultancy role. Alan, a dear friend and colleague, was presenting a marketing concept to three executives from a large corporation. As I had heard the presentation before, I used the time to closely observe the body language of our targets. It was an illuminating experience. Without saying much at all, they each clearly expressed a willingness – even desire – to accept the content of the presentation. It was all there, in their eyes, their body positions and the modulation of their verbally non-committal responses. As we left the meeting I assured Alan that this company would support the project. They did in fact call a few days later and accept our proposal.

If possible, arrange to have a colleague present at your renegotiation meeting to observe your counterpart's facial and body cues. It is astonishing how easily such hints can be observed and interpreted. Professional card players do this well. The good and successful ones analyse the body and facial signals of their opponents not on guessing what cards they might have in their hands.

Should you mention other offers?

It is quite acceptable to intimate that it would be in the company's best interests to sign quickly. Depending on whether you hold a hilltop or a valley position in the relationship (discussed earlier), you may want to consider alluding to other companies interested in taking over this contract. In business, sellers rarely let a potential buyer know that they are the only customer in the market for a product. But take particular care in using this strategy, as you risk offending a sponsor with whom you have had a good relationship, or as a worse case scenario, having them withdraw from the negotiation altogether.

Before attempting this ploy be sure that you thoroughly understand your negotiating counterpart and your relative positions.

One constant source of annoyance to me during renegotiation was the early introduction of competitor interest in the sponsorship property – often the opening statement would be, 'Your competitor has offered us more money to sign with them.' This immediately shifts the focus of discussions to a bidding war. Such organisations had played their trump card too early, placing themselves at a distinct disadvantage. My answer was, 'OK, why don't you sign with them?' This statement negated any bargaining power they previously held. The fatal flaw in their preparation was that they had failed to understand that it was my policy not to involve my company in bidding wars for sponsorships. Negotiation is a serious process. Know when in that process to employ this type of strategy and when to remain silent.

On the other hand, don't underestimate your bargaining power – your position could be stronger than you think; if your homework reveals that you hold the high ground, then by all means use it.

Summarise your agreement

Once agreement has been reached, draw up a simple schedule, detailing all promises made by each side. Agree on the order in which actions will be implemented, and when you return to your organisation, draft a letter to your sponsor that states the terms and conditions in plain, unambiguous language. This is just extra insurance against the possibility that you each left the meeting believing something different had been agreed.

FROM THE EXPERTS

When do you begin renegotiating with your sponsored parties?

- ❖ 'I always start midway through the final term.'
- ❖ 'I like to commence renegotiating a deal at least six months before expiry.'
- ❖ 'I prefer to be cautious. If I left it until the last minute, the property might surprise me with some request or condition that would throw the whole thing wide open and I'd be forced to make a decision too quickly. These things can't be rushed.'
- ❖ 'I like to start fresh negotiations before contracts conclude.'

Who instigates renegotiation?

- ❖ 'We instigate renegotiation. Rarely does the request come from the sponsored party.'
- ❖ 'We flag contracts that have only six months to go and make a decision on whether to renegotiate or not. Those we choose to renegotiate, we contact to get the ball rolling. We usually give organisations six months notice if we are not going to renew.'
- ❖ 'Almost invariably it is we who take the initiative. We have a system that allows us to see when a contract is coming due and we are usually aware of it [the expiry date] well before the sponsored property starts to think about it.'

LESSONS TO TAKE FROM THIS CHAPTER

- ❖ Renegotiation must be approached seriously.
- ❖ Using the knowledge you have gained of the sponsor through working with them, develop a deal they can't refuse.
- ❖ Prepare evidence of how well you have performed so far.
- ❖ Use the renegotiation process to up-sell your sponsor to a higher place in the hierarchy.
- ❖ You have negotiating skills – use them.

SUGGESTED RESEARCH EXERCISES

Observe two people in conversation. Stand far enough away that you can't hear what they are saying but can see all of their actions.
- ❖ Are they in agreement or is there some disharmony?
- ❖ What is each person saying non-verbally?
- ❖ Can you identify any signals they are sending:
- ❖ for example:
  - o are their arms crossed?
  - o eyes averted?
  - o Bodies turned away?

Try this again when you are talking to a colleague. Observe the body language more than the words being spoken. Are you receiving a clearer message verbally or non-verbally?

When someone approaches you asking for a favour, negotiate with them for something in return and aim for a win–win outcome.

- ❖ Were they surprised that you negotiated with them?
- ❖ Were they surprised that you asked for something in return?
- ❖ Did the process proceed in a natural, unforced way?
- ❖ Were you successful in achieving that win–win goal?
- ❖ Did you or the other party concede any points?
- ❖ How do you feel about your negotiation skills now – are there weaknesses that need to be addressed with further practice?

Seventeen

Exiting the maze

'Success is the sum of small efforts,
repeated day in and day out . . .'
ROBERT COLLIER

I hope you have enjoyed the journey through the maze. As you exit with its blueprint in hand, take some time to look back at all the hints, clues and signposts that kept you moving forward, and the guide ropes that prevented you from falling. You can now identify what to do and what not to do, what to pursue with passion and what to avoid. The faceless person at a company's sponsorship helm, the sponsorship manager who controls both the purse strings and your aspirations, is no longer a mystery.

Please, if you are serious about sponsorship, read this book again and refer to it often. It is too easy to slip back into old habits. There will always be others who hold more information than you and that is their strength. By reading this book and putting its advice into practice, you have gained some of their power and given yourself a competitive edge over rival organisations – and even over the sponsorship manager.

Throughout this book, the sections called 'From the experts' have provided pearls of wisdom – some possibly straight from the mouth of someone you will one day negotiate with. At the end of my survey, I asked the managers to provide one hint that would help a novice in their quest to obtain support. Once again, their tips are provided at the conclusion of this chapter; disregard them at your peril.

Although I wish this book could guarantee that sponsors will beat a path to your door and lay untold wealth at your feet, we both know it can't and that only hard work can yield that outcome. It will, however, differentiate you from the mob; the professionalism and insights you have learned and will demonstrate in your negotiations will set you apart as being someone worth meeting. The real benefit you will have gained from this book is that you can now see the maze clearly laid out, track its various corridors and operate from that insider knowledge. While reading it you will have slowly shifted your thinking and altered the paradigms that might have held you or your organisation back.

There you have it. You're armed and dangerous – go get 'em.

I'll leave you with the words of one of the thousands of sponsorship seekers I interviewed over many years. What this person said proved to me that the wise walk among us disguised as ordinary people. I have endeavoured to live my life according to these words and I hope they provide an inspiration to you in your quest for sponsorship funding:

'There are no losers – only winners who give up too soon.'

LAST WORDS FROM THE EXPERTS

- ❖ 'Always be well groomed and positive in your approach.'
- ❖ 'Don't ever be late for meetings. The cardinal sin, of course, is not to turn up at all.'
- ❖ 'Don't promise something you can't provide.'
- ❖ 'Be prepared. There's nothing more frustrating than sitting in a meeting with someone who doesn't know their subject, knows nothing about us and doesn't have any of the paperwork I need.'
- ❖ 'Dress for success.'
- ❖ 'If you are renegotiating and don't know an answer, don't make it up.'
- ❖ 'Remember, honesty will build a relationship more than all of the promises in the world. Smile and be honest.'
- ❖ 'Make the sponsorship manager your friend.'

Case study: Approaching sponsors Mike Bowen style

Most of the advice in this book has been theoretical – a 'do this, then this and you'll get that' approach. Now I would like to present to you a person who has made an art form of seeking sponsorship, a man whose technique in securing and maintaining sponsorships is close to flawless. I have already mentioned that he is someone to emulate, but I believe that by devoting several pages to him I can give you not only a valuable insight into the sponsorship process, but a model against which you can measure your own strengths and weaknesses and those of anyone representing your organisation.

Mike Bowen is not alone in his abilities. There are several people I could have used for this purpose, but when I had to settle on one, Mike seemed to stand out. I first met him about twenty years ago and since then our relationship has evolved from being strangers to acquaintances to friends. Interestingly, as I began to write this case study I realised that I had no real idea how this change in our relationship occurred or why I so readily accepted him and his proposals. All I can say is that his professionalism meant there was never a moment of doubt, discontent or irritation in my dealings with him. But I assure you there were plenty of others who made up for that!

I decided that the best way to present Mike to you was to interview him at length to develop an insight into the man and his attitudes to the work of sponsorship seeking. So, over coffee and lunch and more coffee, we chatted and this is the transcript of that conversation. I'll let you judge from where Mike derives his success. Is he really the consummate professional? Or does he, as I sometimes suspect, wield some supernatural power – a legacy from a hidden leprechaun ancestry?

MIKE TURNER: IF YOU CAN CAST YOUR MIND WAY BACK TO OUR FIRST MEETING, WHAT DID YOU DO TO GAIN AN APPOINTMENT WITH ME? ALSO, WHAT WERE YOUR EXPECTATIONS OF THE MEETING?

Mike Bowen: I certainly do remember our primary meeting, because before it I had a lot of work to do. I didn't have a full handle on who was who and how your company worked in terms of sponsorship. My initial problem-solving dilemma was threefold.

My first objective was the personal thing – to find out who was the ultimate decision maker in your organisation. Next I looked for an avenue in, a contact within your company or someone who we both knew who could plug me straight into that person. And finally I had to find an angle that would make my offering attractive to you.

I never approach anyone directly. I always look for someone I know, or who someone else knows, to get me an introduction to the decision maker. I've been in Australia over 38 years and in that time almost every business deal I've done has been on referral – cold calls have been virtually non-existent. It all gets down to knowing people who know people. By making a cold approach, instantly we have a barrier – no matter how big or small, a barrier exists. If you approach with a recommendation, you don't have to worry about barriers. It was much easier to call you and say, 'One of your colleagues has referred me and could I possibly have a few minutes of your time to meet with you? All I really want to do is sit down and maybe have a coffee and see if we have any areas of mutual interest.'

As I'd had dealings with one of your Guinness colleagues through various functions held in the Irish community, I asked him to put in a good word for me and arrange an appointment so that I could meet you. That taken care of, I set about planning my presentation, which involved asking for support for a book of poetry I'd written.

My book, Fantasy Amber, was all about the demon drink and drink driving. I thought that as you were the sponsorship manager for a brewery, you might have been eager to sponsor something that contained references to the product you brewed. Call it Irish logic, call it naivety, but common sense should have told me that a brewery would not want to sponsor anything that was saying 'Hey, hold on a sec . . . the drink's no good for you.'

I should have had my act together and thought my presentation through more clearly. I could have been more persuasive, but when it was all said and done, my proposal did not match your company's requirements. That's plainly why I didn't get what I was seeking. The answer obviously came back 'no'. Again, common sense told me that it was a 'no' for commercial reasons and for that particular proposal. However, you didn't say, 'Hey Bowen, don't come back again – not even with an entirely different proposal.' I think this is where a lot of people get themselves into a bother. They run off trying to do a deal with forty-five other different sponsors. I believe they should be trying to build up relationships with a select few. Those they have built up an information base on; those with which they have an already made contact, and whose faces and names they know. Build up a trust thing – that's the name of the game.

MT: IF YOU HAD NOT HAD A CONTACT AT CUB, WHAT WOULD YOU HAVE DONE?

MB: Well, if I hadn't had a contact I would have found some system of getting in. It is never good enough to knock at a door. Because knocking on the door means a cold call. There has to be some referral or some mutual understanding. It gets back to desire. If I need and desire something you have, I've got to adapt to you. If you remember our first meeting, initially it was, 'Sorry, we won't do the book.' But when I went back the second time, it wasn't a cold call. I'd already made a contact. If I hadn't got a contact I would simply have done more research. I would have found a way in. Nothing would stop me. I would have found someone who knew you and I would have made that contact.

MT: HOW DO YOU BUILD THOSE RELATIONSHIPS?

MB: In my business – financial management – I approach clients to persuade them to do multi-million-dollar business with me. Initially they might say, 'Hell, we don't know this bloke from Adam.' They could probably tell me, 'You've got Buckley's hope of getting our business at the moment as we don't know you.' So how can I solve this situation? The answer is that I have to build a relationship with them before they will trust me. That, to me, is the linchpin – the most important factor. My philosophy is that the company I represent, the money I handle and the people I deal with are all too precious for me to just pass over and treat in an offhand manner.

So I set about building a relationship. That involves lots of meetings with the necessary consumption of copious cups of coffee that, no doubt, batter my poor kidneys along the way. As my intentions are honourable and if I'm really determined, we will find mutually agreeable grounds on which to do business – we will both profit from our association. When you are working with relationships, be it in business or the sponsorship area, the most important thing is that it has to be a 50–50 deal, because remember, I can – we all can – give our business to anyone. There are three and a half to four million people out there who would be happy to take my business – so I can ask, 'Why should I give it to you?'

On the same plane, if you are working on a sponsorship deal and you are the sponsorship manager, you can give your funding to anyone. What you want is the best value for your company, and I, as the Sponsorship property, have to be prepared to give you that. If I can't provide the value you are looking for, there should be no offence taken on my part. You've got to do your job. It simply means that I haven't done my job well enough to be rewarded with acceptance of my proposal.

MT: HOW DO YOU THINK A SPONSORSHIP MANAGER RECEIVES YOUR TYPE OF APPROACH? YOU SAID EARLIER THAT YOU JUST WANTED TO HAVE COFFEE AND A CHAT TO SEE IF WE HAD AREAS OF MUTUAL INTEREST. HOW DO YOU THINK I FELT ABOUT THAT, AND DID YOU THINK I WOULD TAKE THE BAIT? AFTER ALL, I MIGHT BE RECEIVING APPROACHES EVERY FEW MINUTES OF THE DAY.

MB: Well, it's certainly not a cold call, yet it's not quite a familiarity thing. By being referred by a friend or colleague and by using their name in the conversation, you are probably more at ease because they would not usually recommend time wasters. Your colleagues are aware of the demands on your time so would only recommend quality people to you. In your position every man and his dog wants a slice of your time. I remember sitting in your office and the fax was going and I asked you how many proposals came in per day. And you said some silly amount and I thought, 'Ha! At least I'm here in front of him, which means he hasn't got time to read those other ones. I've got the floor and at the moment I'm his major concern.'

Had I made a cold approach to you, I would have been just one more name on a never-ending list or on a fax that came through with all the others. By being recommended – and making sure your colleague mentioned my name to you before I called you–I gave myself the opportunity of being elevated to the top of the pile of calls you received on that day. Of the, say, twenty to thirty calls you received in sponsorship in one day, how many came from people with recommendations? Not many, I'll bet you. It's an avenue by which you can cut down the odds and cut out 90 per cent of other hopefuls. That's the difference – separating out the wheat from the chaff if you like.

I think what happens when you approach somebody the way I approached you is that you are seen as different – not just someone who wants something specific. I imagine that in your position you would approach an interview with the mindset, 'Here's somebody who wants to take advantage of me.' In my case, I wanted to see how you felt about my book and if there were any areas in which you could help me. It was a case of my seeing you mainly to gain your advice and to start the relationship-building process. It was not about, 'Well, you're in sponsorship and you control a large budget, give me some of it.'

You've probably interviewed countless people who think there is an element of entitlement: to receive sponsorship funding from you is their God-given right and a knock-back is an offence against them. I've argued with a lot of organisations that have asked me to represent them in seeking sponsorship funds – charities, sporting clubs, the music industry and the like. They would ask me continually to approach you for support. I used to say, 'You have to know when enough is enough, and you have to know that Mike's company is being swamped with requests. Put yourself in that position. How would you feel? He can't sponsor everything and he can't sponsor any more than budgets and company policies allow.'

MT: THE NEXT TIME YOU CAME TO ME YOU HAD A GOOD, SOLID PROPOSAL, BUT IT WAS ONE I COULD ONLY PARTIALLY HELP YOU OUT WITH DUE TO THE NATURE OF THE PROPERTY. BUT IT WAS A START.

MB: When I approached you at that time I had done my homework and it was a well-planned effort. My approach was, 'Mike, can I have a few minutes of your time to have a talk with you? I've got a proposal that I believe offers real benefit to your company.'

My proposal required you to agree to three requests and the upshot was that I wanted permission to use the name 'Foster's Lager' in a song, your help in securing interest for an England/Ireland music tour from the

Courage Brewery in London, and some posters and clothing for the lads in the band.

You recall the Flying Wallabies were about to release an album that had a song on it they had written called 'I've got to have a Guinness'. I knew that the Guinness organisation in Australia would not be interested as I'd done a fair bit of groundwork on them. So I called the lads in the band together and suggested that if we re-recorded the song and adjusted the lyrics so the song was 'I've got to have a Foster's Lager', we might have a chance to get Mike Turner to support us. We were simply looking for your blessing and showing you that we didn't want anything at this stage. We were actually just offering your company something for nothing.

MT: YOU APPEAR TO PUT A LOT OF EFFORT INTO BUILDING STRONG RELATIONSHIPS RATHER THEN SIMPLY GOING FOR THE DOLLARS. IS THIS IMPORTANT TO YOU?

MB: Well, absolutely. As you know, that tour went ahead and was very successful. I presented you with lots of evidence of the work we had done for the Foster's brand in return for the faith and support you gave us. From there I believe you could see that I was honest and would deliver the benefits I promised. And here we are fifteen years later, and you are no longer at CUB. But we still talk regularly. I believe that if I rang you tomorrow and asked you to have a drink, I'm pretty sure you'd come. There's a responsibility. It's not 'I want, I want, I want'. It's also, 'Is there anything I can do?' And there's a huge obligation to stick with them though the good times and the low points. It's not all about picking up a cheque. The rewards are greater than the cheque.

You continued to support my proposals over the years but you always supported me based on company policy. I had to earn support through the merits of my proposals, not through our blossoming friendship. Again I say it's a trust thing. That's what lasting relationships are based on. If you lose the trust of a sponsor, you lose their support forever. I can't understand anyone who is not appreciative and doesn't have the good sense to want to work for their sponsors. They may as well run a sharp knife over their throats, because metaphorically that is exactly what they are doing. If you get a bad reputation in this business then you are finished.

MT: HOW DO YOU LOOK AFTER YOUR SPONSORS?

MB: People often forget to say 'thank you' and that is so important. They think that because it's a big company with lots of money they don't need to show their appreciation. You were an awkward person to deal with because you were so busy. If you remember when the Fureys came here, there was such a drama getting you to have lunch with them. Once we found the right time for you, you had great fun. We got you a poster signed by all the boys, even the roadies. [I have it framed in my home office.] I wanted you to feel part of the experience so that you knew what you were putting your money into. Make the people feel important and that what they are doing is appreciated. I always ask, 'What's the best way that I can ensure that people remember me?'

MT: HOW MUCH TIME WOULD YOU DEVOTE, ON AVERAGE, TO PREPARATION FOR AN APPROACH TO A SPONSOR?

MB: Well, the quality of the response you'll get back will depend on the quality of information you have on the people you're dealing with. And it has to be appropriate. If, for instance, I was looking for $100 000 from you, I would have had to put in a hell of a lot more time and a hell of a lot better presentation than I did when asking for much less. I understood that you were dealing with the Caulfield Cup and the Grand Prix and that if you were dealing with major stuff, I was a fairly small fish. It has to be appropriate for what you're doing and what you want. OK, say you're from a kindergarten and you're looking for $40 000, you have to look at it from a professional point of view. People will say, 'Look, I'll knock at the door and see if I can get $5000 off them or I can get perhaps $10 000.' Well, you can't do that.

Sponsors can give their money to anyone and they want to make sure that this guy who's looking for their money knows what he's about. It's very important for people to understand that sponsorship managers are terribly hassled and everyone wants their quid. You have to have a different approach. It can't be a callous approach. Most people come from the begging tack – with their hand out. Now when I came to you with the song, I was giving you something – that was a bit of a twist.

MT: WHAT INFORMATION DO YOU BELIEVE IS VITAL TO HAVE BEFORE MAKING AN APPROACH TO A SPONSOR?

MB: I would be out there for a week before the meeting, talking to everyone – people who know people who know people – finding out who the important players are, what the company needs are, what the company image is, and I'd make the presentation based on that.

MT: IF AT FIRST YOU DON'T SUCCEED, WHAT THEN?

MB: I never take no for an answer. You know me, I don't believe in such a thing. Success is an attitude. For example, there is one sponsorship manager who is a monumental problem. I don't think he likes me. In business not everyone likes everyone else – that's just the way it is. But I tell you, if I needed $10 000 from him, I guarantee I'd get it.

MT: HAS THE SPONSORSHIP FIELD CHANGED SINCE YOU STARTED FIFTEEN YEARS AGO? IF SO, HOW?

MB: Companies have got a lot slicker. They are targeting more. For people on my side of the fence it means getting back to doing the research. The only way you win battles is by knowing your enemy. The presentation must be slicker now. I don't think the money has diminished; I think they are working smarter and we are working smarter. Everything is more streamlined. There are a lot of people out there looking for the same sponsorship dollars.

So again it comes down to research and approach. It is not good enough to go in saying, 'We've got a worthy charity, give us X dollars.' It's a matter of going in and saying, 'Here's a business plan and it would be great for your company to be seen to be helping out with this. If we work together we'll achieve something worthwhile. There's a tremendous benefit for your company and a benefit for us.' It may mean that you don't get the whole loaf. But going in looking for $100 000 and coming out with nothing and calling the company a pack of shits is not a good way of doing business. Going in there and getting a slice of bread today and two slices next week and perhaps half a loaf in a few months' time – after six months you will have a loaf of bread. And you've built a relationship on scraps of bread.

MT: PRESUMABLY WHEN YOU FIRST STARTED YOU MADE SOME MISTAKES, LIKE NOT CONSIDERING THE BREWERY'S STANCE ON YOUR ANTI-ALCOHOL POETRY. WHAT ARE SOME OF THE IMPORTANT LESSONS YOU'VE LEARNED?

MB: You're dead right. I walked in to you and said I've written a book of poems and one of them is an anti-drinking. I shot a huge hole in my foot. But I would never look at anything as a mistake – it's an experience you build on. Go back and revamp, and then go back and revamp, and then go back and revamp until you've got it right. There's no 'no' in my vocabulary. If you give me a 'no' it's just that I haven't got the things you need. I haven't refined my presentation directly for you. If you said, 'And don't you ever come back', then I'd get my secretary to call you. People have to realize that they should not take 'no' offensively. I've learned that much.

MT: WHAT INTANGIBLES DO YOU GET FROM YOUR WORK IN SPONSORSHIP?

MB: There is a lot of satisfaction working with people in sponsorship. I use it as a network system to a point. I met a lot of people and made a lot of business contacts. Enormous satisfaction.

MT: WHAT IS YOUR ADVICE TO ANYONE OUT THERE SEEKING SPONSORS FOR THE FIRST TIME?

MB: [and this will do nicely as our summary] Look for sponsors that suit the event or occasion you want supported. When you find them, don't go anywhere near them until you find somebody somewhere who can connect you to the right person in the right way. Not just anyone in the company, but the 'yes' person – the one who makes the decisions.

Never, never give up until you have exhausted all avenues and that 'yes' person has said 'no'. Accept that it's going to happen at some stage and pick yourself up and continue with the search. Remember to keep the lines of communication open – you can always go back at a later stage.

When you find a sponsor, always be honest. Tell the truth and work at forming a bond with them. Build that bond on trust and respect – the more you give, the more you receive in return. That's my advice. It has worked for me. It can work for others if they are prepared to make a real go of it. No doesn't mean no, it just means you've got the presentation wrong. Get the best person to do the presentation. And research, research, research!

A Showbag of Samples

In the following pages there is a series of letters you might need to use in your journey through the maze. They will act as a guide if you are unsure of the correct form of letter to send in a given circumstance.

I have also included a simple contract which will suffice in most cases, and an example of the layout of a basic media release.

In the showbag

1. Simple proposal letter

2. Letter authorising a professional agent to act on your behalf

3. Letter confirming details

4. Simple contract

5. Sample media release

6. Letter offering to renegotiate

1. Simple proposal letter

Actors Playhouse
2001 Stallone Street, Gibsonville 9054

12 November 2013

Mr. J Toffee,
Chairperson,
Fruit Gum Company,
1910 Sugar Lane,
Gibsonville. 9054.

Dear Mr. Toffee,

Our repertory company is producing the world-acclaimed play *Everything you wanted to know about sponsorships* by the multi- award-winning playwright Anne Expert. We are offering you the opportunity to sponsor this exciting play, which is booked to run for a five- week season beginning on 1 June 2002. Test audiences who have seen the play have provided very encouraging feedback, and we are extremely confident that its run will extend well beyond its initial five weeks.

We request a sum of $20,000 in cash. This will be allocated to our advertising and promotions budget and will offset the costs of props and scenery. In return for your generous support we offer the following benefits:

- ❖ major sponsor status with acknowledgements in all advertising, posters, tickets and all other printed material
- ❖ ten front-row seats at the premiere, including ten invitations to the premiere's after-show party
- ❖ four front-row tickets to every performance, including extensions
- ❖ display opportunities for your products in the theatre foyer
- ❖ product sampling opportunities to the nightly full houses (578 patrons per night).

Actors Playhouse is proud to have provided its sponsors exclusive marketing opportunities with previous productions held in this theatre. For example, our last two plays, *I Fell from the Empire State Building by Eileen Dover and The Horticulturalist by Teresa Green*, increased sales for their respective sponsors. I can provide you with a breakdown of the sales increases achieved during the run of each play should you wish to see them.

We look forward to an early favourable reply so that we can commence planning what we believe will be a most exciting and fruitful partnership. Please contact me if you have any further enquires.

Regards,

Basil Plumm - Jamm

Basil Plumm-Jamm
Executive Director

2. Letter authorising a professional agent to act on your behalf

Actors Playhouse
2001 Stallone Street, Gibsonville 9054

12 November, 2013

Mr. B. Agent,
The Sponsorship Consultancy,
2468 Motorway,
Gibsonville. 9054.

Dear Mr. Agent,

This letter is to advise you of your appointment as sponsorship agent for our organisation. You are, as of this date, duly authorised to negotiate, discuss and in any other way communicate with companies and individuals in matters relating to securing sponsorship funding for Actors Playhouse.

Your powers will include negotiating agreements, accepting or rejecting offers and entering into contracts that are binding on Actors Playhouse, provided that such agreements are not deemed illegal or morally and ethically at odds with the character and policy of Actors Playhouse.

You are to act in such a manner as you see fit to accomplish the goals and objectives set out by this organisation in the pursuit of sponsorship funding.

The authority granted to you in this letter will expire in twelve months from the date of this letter.

We look forward to a mutually fruitful relationship.

Regards,

Basil Plumm - Jamm

Basil Plumm-Jamm
Executive Director

3. Letter confirming details

You may recall that I advised you to return to your organization after successful talks with a sponsor and draft a letter detailing the terms agreed. Here is the sort of letter you might send. Once this has been returned countersigned by the person with whom your discussions were held, you can be confident that both parties fully understand and agree to the terms and conditions.

Actors Playhouse
2001 Stallone Street, Gibsonville 9054

10 December, 2013

Mr. J Toffee,
Chairperson,
Fruit Gum Company,
1910 Sugar Lane,
Gibsonville. 9054.

Dear James,

This letter is to confirm the details of our discussions at the Gentleperson's Club today.

You agreed that your company, Fruit Gum Company, will sponsor Actors Playhouse for a three-year period commencing on 1st January, 2014 and expiring on 31st December, 2017.

We also agreed that Fruit Gum Company would provide the sum of $25 000 in each year of the agreement and would be the major sponsor of Actors Playhouse during the period of our agreement. All benefits to be provided by Actors Playhouse will be detailed in the formal contract.

If the above meets with your understanding of our negotiations, would you please sign this letter and return it to me. On receipt we will forward all details to our solicitors for drafting the contract.

It was a pleasure to have your company again today. I will see you soon with contracts in hand.

Kind regards,

Basil

Basil Plumm - Jamm

4. Simple contract

This is a simple, basic contract that can be drafted by either party to a sponsorship agreement. It should contain all of the information required so that you and your sponsor each understand your obligations under the agreement. If you are not sure about the meaning or effect of any clause, get a legal expert to run their trained eye over the document. Never sign anything about which you are unsure.

CONTRACT FOR SPONSORSHIP

Fruit Gum Company of 1910 Sugar Lane, Gibsonville 9054, agrees to sponsor Actors Playhouse of 2001 Stallone Street, Gibsonville 9054, specifically for its production of *Everything you wanted to know about sponsorships* by Anne Expert.

The play is scheduled to run for a five-week season. The premiere performance date is 1 June 2002. The planned final performance is to be held on 5 September, 2014. Should this season be extended, the Fruit Gum Company will continue as major sponsor with all the benefits intact at no extra cost.

Fruit Gum Company will pay Actors Playhouse the sum of $20,000 cash ('the sponsorship fee') on receipt of an invoice after signing of this agreement.

In return for the sponsorship fee, both Fruit Gum Company and Actors Playhouse agree to all the obligations and conditions set out below:
1. major sponsor status with acknowledgements in all advertising, posters, tickets and all other printed material
2. ten front-row seats at the premiere, including ten invitations to the after-show party
3. four front-row tickets to every performance, including extensions
4. display opportunities for your products in the theatre foyer
5. product sampling rights for the whole season.

Actors Playhouse acknowledges that no other company or individual in direct competition with Fruit Gum Company can or will be granted sponsorship, signage or advertising rights to the play *Everything you wanted to know about sponsorships.*

This contract may not be modified in any way unless agreed in writing and signed by both parties. This document and all attachments constitute the entire agreement and bind and benefit both parties.

Signed for and on behalf of **Fruit Gum Company**

Signed: *J. Toffee*
Witnessed: *Coco Jellybean*
Date: 1St January, 2013

Signed for and on behalf of **Actors Playhouse**

Signed: *Basil Plumm - Jamm*
Witnessed: *H. Hamlet*
Date: 1St January, 2013

5. Sample media release

**FRUIT GUM COMPANY
MEDIA RELEASE**
Fruit Gum Company 1910 Sugar Lane Gibsonville 9054
Date: 21st January 2013

YUMMY GUMS AND ACTORS PLAYHOUSE
– A SWEET MIX

Fruit Gum Company today took a leadership role in the arts by becoming an Official Sponsor of Actors Playhouse. Under the Yummy Gums brand, the company will be supporting the forthcoming production *Everything you wanted to know about sponsorships.*

'Fruit Gum Company is very excited to be an official sponsor of this unique production,' said the company chairperson, James Toffee. 'We are very proud to be associated with Actors Playhouse and Yummy Gums and our entire family of brands seemed like a perfect fit.'

As a sponsor, Yummy Gums will help ensure the production is a major success by providing the funds necessary to engage award-winning actors Douglas Michael and Roberta Julian in the lead roles. Ironically, both Julian and Michael began their acting careers in minor roles in Actors Playhouse productions.

'The Fruit Gum Company sponsorship will make a significant impact on the quality of Actors Playhouse productions. The support will greatly assist in the development of new talent by exposing young actors to the work of such gifted thespians as Roberta Julian and Douglas Michael,' said Actors Playhouse executive director Basil Plumm-Jamm.

Everything you wanted to know about sponsorships is scheduled for a five-week season commencing with the premiere performance on June 1, 2014. 'Although the play is booked for a standard five-week run,' added Plumm-Jamm, 'interest from our patrons points to a lengthy extended season.'

Fruit Gum Company's family of products is manufactured to the highest standards and contains no less than 25% real fruit juice. They are a treat for everyone at any time and have remained a family favourite for over fifty years.

In addition to supporting Actors Playhouse, Fruit Gum Company is also involved with the community at a more grassroots level. It assists local arts, education, culture and sports initiatives, actively encouraging its 500 employees to supplement the company's efforts through volunteer work within the communities they serve.

Release contact:
Verity Newsworthy: Fruit Gum Company
Phone: 555 55455 / Fax: 555 55454
E-mail: vnewsworthy@sweettooth.com

Actors Playhouse contact:
Basil Plumm-Jamm, Executive Director
Phone: 555 33233 / Fax: 555 33232
E-mail: basilpj@hamitup.net

6. Letter offering to renegotiate

When you take the initiative and want to begin renegotiation talks, this is the type of letter you should send. Note that as you probably know this person quite well now, the more formal titles and forms of address can be dropped.

Actors Playhouse
2001 Stallone Street, Gibsonville 9054

20 February, 2014

Mr. J. Toffee,
Chairperson,
Fruit Gum Company,
1910 Sugar Lane,
Gibsonville. 9054.

Dear James,

As you are aware, our three-year sponsorship contract is due to expire in six months from the date of this letter. I would like to express my desire to begin negotiations in an effort to ensure the smooth continuation of our relationship.

I have prepared a new proposal that contains some exciting and radical ideas. I am sure that your company will continue to benefit from our association, particularly with the new developments that our organisation will introduce during the next two years.

May I suggest that we meet on Friday next at 1 p.m. in the Sports Bar at the Gentleperson's Club on Deal Street, Gibsonville? I hope you will find this arrangement convenient.

I look forward to hearing from you,

Regards,

Basil

Glossary of terms

This is a list of industry terms and definitions that are used frequently by sponsorship managers. If you take the time to familiarise yourself with the terminology, you will be able to keep up with and understand what the sponsorship manager is saying during the course of an interview or negotiation. Understanding the definitions will also demonstrate to sponsorship managers that you are a prepared and professional representative of your organisation.

AFFINITY MARKETING	Marketing strategies that allow consumers to closely align themselves with certain organisations. For example, where a bank is sponsoring say a sporting organisation, it may offer fans credit cards which are branded with the logo of the fan's team. When they use the club card, their team benefits.
AGENT	See "consultant"
ALLIANCE	Arrangement where two or more parties agree to join forces in the pursuit of a common goal.
AMBUSH MARKETING	A non-sponsor's efforts to align their company or brands with an event (to which they are not associated) and create the illusion of being a bona fide sponsor. This is done to gain some benefit from the appearance of being allied to the event: an unwitting consumer could be persuaded to buy products from a firm that is perceived as being a sponsor of a property to which it has no valid connection.
APPAREL	Any form of clothing featuring logos or brands of sponsors. Items including caps, T-shirts and jackets are produced by either the sponsor or event organisers and are sold or given away.
AUDIENCE	Target market segment or individuals at whom the sponsorship is aimed, for

	example, fans of a particular football team or patrons of the opera or some other branch of the arts.
AWARENESS	Sponsors may wish to use an event or property to create and maintain brand awareness in the minds of consumers. The event is used to bring the sponsor or its products to the attention of the consumer and, with continued brand imagery, aids 'top of mind' brand recall.
BANNER	Sign carrying event or sponsor messages; usually made from vinyl material. These transportable and reusable signs are used at events as either temporary signage or where existing signage requires an extra boost. A cost-effective and simple way of providing sponsor identification.
BARRIER TO ENTRY	By signing a binding agreement with a sponsorship property, a business can exclude competitors from associating with that property. The firm has effectively raised an impenetrable barrier that a competitor cannot penetrate until such time as the existing agreement between the sponsor and property ends.
BEER RIGHTS	Exclusive rights bestowed on a brewery allowing it alone to sell its beer products at events. Similar rights can relate to any product category.
BENEFITS	Aspects of the agreement from which both parties derive tangible and intangible advantage, such as (for the property) the funding required to enable it to stage an event or (for the sponsor) product awareness or increased sales.
BRAINSTORMING	Bringing people into a forum for discussion where it is hoped that ideas will be generated, problems will be solved and new opportunities will be identified. The general rules for brainstorming are that no

	idea is stupid, and none should be discarded until considered and debated by the entire team.
BRAND LOYALTY	Results from the consumer's involvement with a brand in a specific product category where liking leads to consistent purchase and usage.
BRAND MARKETING	Process of identifying a product as distinct from others of its type by using brand names, designs, symbols or terms. For example, Heinz Baked Beans and the slogan 'Beanz meanz Heinz' differentiates that brand from every other baked-bean product in the market.
BRANDING	Identifying a property, event, organisation, idea, product or service by giving it a name, a distinctive symbol, some terminology, a specific design or another feature that distinguishes it from other offerings
BUDGET	Amount of support, usually in terms of dollars, that is allocated by sponsors for their sponsorship support activities. The sponsorship budget is usually appropriated annually.
BUDGET CONSTRAINTS	The most common reason given by sponsors as to their inability to take up proposals. This could be factual, as most organisations allocate their budgets early in a new financial year, but sponsorship managers may also use it as a time-saving measure when they don't want to accept a submission. Here they will send a pro-forma letter that saves time rather than explaining in full detail the true reasons for non-acceptance.
CAPTIVE MARKET	Market where all consumers are forced to use a particular product or service, or go without. For example, where a company has product exclusivity at a venue, patrons will have to use that sponsor's product as there are no alternatives.

CHARTER	Code of conduct by which an organization conducts its day-to-day affairs.
CHERRY PICKING	Situation where a sponsor will select the best available property from a pool of properties. For example, if a sponsor is seeking to sponsor a football club, they will consider all of the football club alternatives and select the organisation that best suits the needs and objectives of their company.
CONSULTANT	Agent or company that specialises in organizing and brokering sponsorship arrangements. They may work on behalf of either party or both parties. The consultant can work for a retainer or a percentage of the sponsorship fee negotiated.
CONSUMER SAMPLING	Provision of a product to consumers free of charge or for a small fee. Some companies may wish to do this via your property and find the method a cost-effective way of conducting a mass sampling exercise on large and small target audiences.
CONTRACT	Legally binding document that sets out all of the benefits and obligations agreed to by parties.
CORPORATE CULTURE	Set of values, beliefs, customs and perceptions about a business that is held and learned by all employees and expressed to the world at large.
CORPORATE SIGNAGE	Sponsor's corporate or company name and logo, not including reference to any brands.
CORPORATE STRATEGY	Flexible plan developed by a company, stating its ultimate goals. It is the company's 'road map' of markets, time and resources that will set it on the path to achieving the goals.
CO-SPONSORS	Pool of companies or brands that sponsor the same event. Although their sponsorship costs vary, they have all paid for the right to

	call themselves sponsors of the event.
CROSS PROMOTION	Sales promotion method that brings together two or more non-competing sponsors who, through the sponsorship, jointly promote their products using a common theme.
DEMOGRAPHICS	Division of markets into groups or segments based on variables that may include age, sex, occupation, income, family size, nationality, education, religion and location.
ENDORSEMENT	Advertising message where a well-known individual or sponsorship property leads consumers to believe that the endorsement reflects their opinions, likes or experiences of a company, brand or service. These types of advertisements are also called 'testimonials'.
EVENT CREATION	Development of an event created to highlight the sponsor's company, products and/or brands. The event may have no real significance in its own right but the sponsor uses its sponsorship of the event purely as a marketing exercise.
EVENT MARKETING	Linking a brand, company, marketing, promotional or advertising strategy to a particular event.
EVENT NICHE	Event that does not have broad marketing or wide consumer appeal but does offer an exclusive market.
EVENT-LINKED ADVERTISING	Any form of sponsor advertising that makes reference to the sponsor's association with an event it has sponsored.
EXCLUSIVITY	Within a defined product or service category, the sponsor is granted the right to recognition as the only product, service or company allied to the property or event.
FAST MOVING CONSUMER GOODS (FMCG)	Products consumed by end users within a relatively short period after purchase. Most goods on supermarket shelves belong to this category of products.

FENCE SIGNAGE	Signs usually identified with sporting events and placed on the inside fences or boundaries or perimeters of event venues or stadia.
FIRST RIGHT OF REFUSAL	Usually negotiated within an initial contract. The sponsor retains the right to renegotiate for the same benefits and conditions enjoyed in the existing arrangement ahead of any other sponsor. This can also be couched in terms of an option to re-sign when the current contract expires.
FLOW ON POTENTIAL	Situation where strong consumer awareness of and affiliation with a sponsoring brand may create increased sales for other brands in the sponsor's portfolio of products.
GOODS IN KIND	Products or services provided as payment in lieu of cash. For example, a company may wish to provide a property with soft drink, which can either be used at social functions, saving the organisation the cost of having to purchase the product, or it is sold to club members. Both methods of consumption will raise revenue for the organisation. Some sponsors refer to this as 'product donation' or a 'contra deal'.
HIERARCHY OF SPONSORS	Ranking of sponsors according to levels of support. It is also utilised to identify sponsors who can be promoted up the hierarchy, and to target future sponsors.
HOSPITALITY	Social and entertainment opportunities that organisations afford to sponsors. They allow networking scope for sponsors and also allow them to cement relations with their sponsored partners.
IMPACT	Intrusiveness of the sponsor's message gauged by the effect on the target audience.

INCENTIVE	Reward for an action. For example, a consumer might buy a sponsor's product and receive a free ticket to an event that is supported by the sponsor.
INFRA-STRUCTURE	All of the support requirements that the sponsor will set in place to ensure the success of the sponsorship. This may include signage, trophies for presentations, sales promotions and promotional staff.
JOINT MAJOR SPONSORS	Two sponsors who each pay a fee in order to gain equal naming rights to an event. This can occur where the sponsorship fee is too great for one sponsor to bear. For example, the Ford Motor Company and the beer brand Heineken have in the past jointly sponsored the Australian Open Tennis Championships held at the Rod Laver Arena, Melbourne Park.
KISS PRINCIPLE	Acronym for 'Keep it simple, stupid'. It is advice to ensure that you don't get overly technical in speech or writing. By keeping your proposal simple, you should maintain the reader's interest and promote understanding.
LICENSING	Where you assign the right to your event, trademark, slogan or logo to your partner in sponsorship to use in promoting the affiliation.
LOGO	Brand mark such as a symbol, design, picture, colour combination or distinctive lettering.
LOGO PROFILE	Awareness and recall of a sponsor's logo among the target audience. If the logo is recognisable and sends the sponsor's message without support wording and other images, then it has a high profile with the target audience.
MAJOR SPONSOR	Sponsor who has paid the highest fee to obtain the right to acknowledgement of their name or brand as the premium sponsor of an event or property. This

	sponsor is also known as the 'naming rights sponsor'.
MARKET SEGMENT	Group of consumers having one or more similar characteristics. A market segment could be 18- to 25-year-old males, who frequent nightclubs at least twice a week and drive cars less than five years old. A sponsor wanting to target this group would refer to it as its 'key market segment'.
MARKET OPPORTUNITY	Any occurrence or thing that may be viewed by a company as offering a competitive advantage.
MASS SAMPLING	Trialling of a product among a large number of potential customers within a relatively short period of time.
MEDIA SPONSOR	Main stream television, cable television, radio, internet companies and print media companies that provide coverage for your property in return for sponsor acknowledgement.
MERCHANDISING	Decoration of a venue or property with a company's branding. Can consist of the placement of banners, point-of-sale material, displays, bunting and flags, and includes all materials that signify the sponsor's ownership or support of an event. The merchandising will be placed according to the sponsor's position in the property's hierarchy of sponsors: the higher tier sponsors get more prominent merchandising.
NAMING RIGHTS	Non-exclusive rights granted to a sponsor which allow them to use the event name in marketing activities according to their designated sponsor level. See also 'Sole naming rights'.
NEGOTIATION	A process where two or more parties, each with individual interests, come together to bargain. Usually the parties will aim for a win–win solution for all.

NICHE MARKET	A small but relatively lucrative market neglected by mass marketers.
'NO' LETTER	Standard or pro-forma letter sent by a target company, in which they politely decline your offer.
OUTDOOR ADVERTISING	Includes posters, bus sides, billboards, illuminated signs, painted signs and outdoor displays.
OVERLAY	Combination of sales promotion tools connected to a sponsorship. For example, several sponsors of the Olympics have over the years run promotional competitions for consumers to win hospitality or ticket packages at the Olympic Games or other Olympic's branded products, merchandise or prizes.
PARTNERSHIP	Mutually beneficial ongoing relationship in which each party has a genuine concern for the welfare and well-being of the other parties.
PERIMETER SIGNAGE	Signage or advertising, either temporary or permanent, that is positioned outside a venue or the site of an event.
PHILANTHROPY	Support for non-profit organisations under either a corporate umbrella or by an individual but where no commercial benefit is sought.
PORTFOLIO	Number, categories and types of properties, events and/or individuals that are sponsored or financially supported by an organisation.
PREMIUMS	Souvenir or give-away items that are produced to highlight a sponsor's association with an event or property, including key rings, pens, notepads etc.
PRESENTATION	Ceremony at which sponsors' representatives are usually afforded the opportunity to make speeches and present awards, cheques or certificates on behalf of their companies.

PRODUCT CATEGORY	Collection of commodities that can be seen by consumers as rational alternatives for each other. For example, one brand of instant coffee can be substituted for another, giving rise to the product category of instant coffee; within that category are all of the brands of instant coffee available in the marketplace.
PRODUCT SALES POTENTIAL	Capacity to sell a product within a given market and the demand from that market for the product.
PROPERTY	Any person, organisation, event, entity or thing that can be sponsored.
PURSE	Entire allocation of funds available for sponsorship spending in a given period.
REACH	A measure of how many people in a sponsor's target market were exposed to an advertising or promotional campaign during a set period of time.
RECALL	Ability of consumers to correctly identify brands in terms of what they read, saw or heard without the aid of reference material while they are answering.
RELATIONSHIP STEPS	Steps and processes in building meaningful and long-term alliances with sponsors.
RELATIONSHIP MARKETING PROGRAM	Program that has been developed to gain the loyalty and support of consumers (repeat purchases of a sponsor's product or service). Frequent-flyer programs are examples of relationship marketing.
RIGHT – FIT TARGET	An estimation that the market available to a company through sponsorship fits the target profile of its product consumers.
SALES PROMOTION	Incentive, usually only utilised in the short term, that entices consumers to purchase a sponsor's product or service.

SALES SCOPE	Total value of potential sales for a brand in a selected market.
SEGMENT	Section of a total market that contains a cluster of consumers, each possessing similar needs. If the total market is motor vehicles, one segment will be for 'people movers'. Here consumers might be those who need a vehicle with the capacity to transport families.
SHOTGUN APPROACH	Ineffective and expensive method of approaching prospective sponsors. An organisation 'aims' in the general direction of a target sponsor by sending out many copies of the same proposal (like the discharge of pellets in a shotgun blast). The hope is that some may be read by a few interested sponsors.
SIGNAGE	Any form of painted or printed material that carries a sponsor's branding, corporate image or logos; used to provide visual stimulation to the patrons of a sponsored event. Such sponsor identification is usually positioned so that a majority of patrons will see it.
SOCIAL MEDIA	Various online technology tools that enable people to communicate easily via the internet to share information and resources. Social media can include text, audio, video, images, podcasts and other multimedia communications. Examples: Twitter, facebook, YouTube etc.
SOLE NAMING RIGHTS	Rights granted to a sponsor to use exclusively the name of an event.
SOLE NAMING RIGHTS - ARENA	Rights granted to a sponsor for their name or brand to be exclusively tied to an arena, venue, stadium or physical property. In naming rights, the length of the deal is very important because it requires both an acceptance and an actual change of behaviour among fans and the media for the

	sponsorship to work.
SOLE SPONSOR	Sponsor who has the desire and resources to support an entire property on its own. This type of sponsor may want to capture the entire market provided by the property or not be overshadowed by other sponsors.
SPONSOR/S	Firm/s or individual/s that provides support in products, services or money to a charitable, fundraising, arts or sports organisations or individuals.
SPONSOR SIGNAGE	Any signage used at an event that features the logos, names, slogans or imagery of official sponsors.
SPONSORED PARTY	Organisation or individual that is the beneficiary of support from a sponsor.
SPONSORSHIP FEE	Amount in cash, product or services paid by companies or individuals wishing to align themselves or their brands to a particular property or event.
SPONSORSHIP PROPERTY	Event, person and/or organisation that has been sponsored by a company.
SWOT ANALYSIS	Situational assessment specifically analysing strengths, weaknesses, opportunities and threats.
SYNERGY	State where the effect of bringing together two or more components to create a course of action is greater than the sum of the individual parts.
TARGET MARKET	Audience made up of groups of people or a market segment to which a particular advertisement expressly appeals.
TRADEMARK	Mark that signifies the link between a product and its proprietor. Trademarks are protected by registration, which reserves exclusive use for the rightful owner.
UNIQUE SELLING PROPOSITION (USP)	Benefit within a sponsorship proposal that can be considered 'unique'; the principal

	persuasive justification in accepting a proposal. Often shortened to 'USP'.
VALUATION	Valuation Analysis of every component within a sponsorship proposal, which ensures that the fee being asked does not exceed the benefits being offered.
WIN - WIN	Final desired outcome in a negotiation, where both parties feel that they have achieved a 'win' situation and neither party has lost on the agreement.
WINDOW SHOPPING	Situation where sponsorship managers may request to read a proposal but are not in the market for such a proposal at that time. As they do not have the immediate intention or inclination to accept your property for sponsorship, they could be merely comparing similar properties.
YELLOW PAGES	Business telephone directory that can be utilised to track down target sponsors.

Printed in Great Britain
by Amazon.co.uk, Ltd.,
Marston Gate.